50 of the Best Strolls, Walks, and Hikes around Carson City

50

of the **Best Strolls, Walks,** and **Hikes** around **Carson City**

By MIKE WHITE

With photographs by MARK VOLLMER

UNIVERSITY OF NEVADA PRESS *Reno & Las Vegas*

University of Nevada Press | Reno, Nevada 89557 USA
www.unpress.nevada.edu
Cover art by Mark Vollmer
All photos are by Mark Vollmer unless otherwise indicated.
Images: page 9 © ufotopix110; page 103 © tinica10; page 159 © mast3r/Adobe Stock;
    page 213 © Salome

LIBRARY OF CONGRESS CATALOGING-IN-PUBLICATION DATA
Names: White, Michael C., 1952– author. | Vollmer, Mark, photographer.
Title: 50 of the best strolls, walks, and hikes around Carson City / by Mike White ;
    with photographs by Mark Vollmer.
Other titles: Fifty of the best strolls, walks, and hikes around Carson City
Description: Reno ; Las Vegas : University of Nevada Press, 2020. | Includes
    index. | Summary: "This guide provides readers with the most precise
    information for a wide range of detailed paths and trails throughout
    the greater Carson City region"—Provided by publisher.
Identifiers: LCCN 2019057913 (print) | LCCN 2019057914 (ebook) |
    ISBN 9781948908665 (paperback) | ISBN 9781948908672 (ebook)
Subjects: LCSH: Walking—Nevada—Carson City Region—Guidebooks. |
    Hiking—Nevada—Carson City Region—Guidebooks. | Trails—Nevada—
    Carson City Region—Guidebooks. | Carson City Region (Nev.)—Guidebooks.
Classification: LCC GV199.42.N32 C378 2020 (print) |
    LCC GV199.42.N32 (ebook) | DDC 796.5109793/57—dc23
LC record available at https://lccn.loc.gov/2019057913
LC ebook record available at https://lccn.loc.gov/2019057914

The paper used in this book meets the requirements of American National Standard
    for Information Sciences—Permanence of Paper for Printed Library Materials,
    ANSI/NISO Z39.48-1992 (R2002).

FIRST PRINTING

Manufactured in the United States of America

Contents

List of Illustrations

Maps

Photos

Acknowledgments

Credit for any of my projects coming to fruition goes to my wife, Robin, whose dedication and sacrifice makes it all possible. Many thanks to Gregg Berggren and Donna Inverson, who provided me with a great deal of quality information about existing and proposed trails throughout the Carson City area. The much-appreciated companionship from fellow hikers during the fieldwork portion included Dal and Candy Hunter, Keith Catlin, Chris Taylor, and Bruce Farenkopf. As usual, Mark Vollmer's wonderful photographs serve as an excellent visual complement to my words, for which I am very grateful. And as usual, Clark Whitethorn and the staff at University of Nevada Press did an exemplary job with their end of the process.

Introduction

Note to Parents

In this present age, many people are becoming less and less involved in the outdoor world, especially children. Certainly, the widespread development and increased accessibility of electronics consumes an enormous amount of the leisure time of young people. While in previous generations parents would shoo their children outside to play, nowadays many parents seem content to allow TV, computers, cell phones, and video games to be their children's babysitters. What little time school-age children do spend outside these days is often limited to organized sports rather than free play. Unfortunately, many physical education (PE) programs have been cut from the school curriculums as well.

The harried nature of family life in the modern era has also wreaked havoc on children's ability to connect with the natural world, especially for families with two working parents or single-parent families. Suburbia seems filled with time-pressed and frazzled parents often appearing to be little more than chauffeurs shuttling their kids from one organized activity to another in an attempt to provide them with every opportunity that presents itself. After school, between soccer practice and music lessons, Mom, Dad, an older sibling, or a sitter makes a pass through the drive-through of a fast-food restaurant, tossing dinner to the kids in the backseat of an SUV or minivan. Little wonder the United States is experiencing a child obesity epidemic, when poor nutrition is combined with minimal physical activity.

Complicating matters even further is the trend of the population moving away from rural and suburban areas to reside in the inner city, where natural and open space is oftentimes less available. In this environment, parents who want their children to experience the great outdoors face an even bigger challenge than their rural and suburban counterparts.

All is not doom and gloom, however, as parents do have the choice to expose their kids to the wonders of the world that exist outside of our man-made enclosures. Fortunately, those of us who live in the greater Carson City area don't have to travel very far to experience the outdoors. But the choice has to be made to prioritize encounters with the natural world outside our back door. While the majority of children are more aware of threats to the environment these days than their parents may have been at the same ages, most kids spend less time actually in that environment than previous

1

generations. Heading outside provides many health benefits, including but not limited to the following:

- **vitamin D:** Healthy children, as well as adults, require a daily dose of this important vitamin, which can be acquired with an exposure of bare skin to sunlight for as short as fifteen minutes per day. An adequate amount of vitamin D is essential to help bodies absorb calcium, which results in the production of healthy bones.
- **immune system boost:** Children who routinely play outside have more active immune systems. While a lot of seemingly responsible parental activity involves minimizing exposure to bacteria in an attempt to keep kids healthy, the opposite is actually true. By exposing children to the outside elements, parents are helping to stimulate their immune systems.
- **exercise:** Outside activities such as hiking, running, riding bikes, pickup games, and playing tag provide a fun way for children to get the necessary exercise they need to be healthy. School-age children are recommended to get an hour of exercise each day. Many children, especially boys, who get labeled hyperactive just might seem less high-strung if allowed to burn off their extra energy playing outside.
- **stress reduction:** Being outdoors can be relaxing and healing to the body, mind, and soul.
- **healthy air:** Unless air pollution is a problem, outside air is generally cleaner than the air inside a building, where recycled and stagnant air accumulates dust particles and other contaminants.
- **heightened senses:** While we use our five senses inside as well as out, being in nature provides a heightened stimulation of our senses.
- **imagination/creativity stimulation:** Kids who participate in free play are able to stimulate their imaginations in ways that electronic stimuli can't replicate.
- **develop problem solving:** Free play also allows children to develop problem-solving skills, as well as improve social skills.
- **discovery:** The natural world is a laboratory for discovery, which most children will naturally find intriguing. Some kids might need some introductory guidance in this regard, but eventually they'll find the outdoors to be filled with myriad opportunities of unearthing some of life's more fascinating wonders.
- **sense of environmental stewardship:** While videos and textbooks can teach kids to be environmentally aware, nothing beats wanting to protect something they find enjoyment in and learn to understand personally.

One of the greatest gifts a parent can give to a child is the freedom to play outside and experience the natural world in a tactile way. Hiking the area's trails is a wonderful way to introduce your kids to the great outdoors. To learn more about this issue, *Last Child in the Woods*, by Richard Louv, is an outstanding resource. Following are some tips for parents when hiking with children:

- Pick an age-appropriate hike that's interesting and fun.
- Remember to make the journey the goal, not the destination. Have reasonable expectations about your child's abilities and desires.
- Pack plenty of snacks and take plenty of rest breaks.
- Bring along a playmate for your child.
- Help kids become good observers of the natural world.
- Plan some activities along the way to keep kids engaged.

Note to Dog Owners

Lots of folks love to bring their dogs along on a hike. Trips that allow dogs on the trail have been identified in the introductory heading of each trip. Some areas don't allow pets at all, others require dogs be on a leash, and still others have no restrictions (although all dogs should be well socialized and under voice control). To keep everyone content in areas where dogs are permitted, here is a list of suggestions:

- **Pick the right trail:** Not only should you obey the regulations and only take your dog on trails where they are allowed, but select a trail suitable for your pet. Make certain your pet is physically up to the challenge. Select a path where the surface won't damage a dog's paws, or invest in a set of dog booties. Make sure plenty of water is available or pack some along for Fido. Avoid trails congested with mountain bikers and equestrians.
- **Maintain control:** Your dog should be leashed where required and under voice control when off leash. He or she should be socially well adjusted, as encounters with humans and other dogs is highly likely on most of the trips in this guide. Don't allow your pet to harass wildlife.
- **Remove feces:** Bring a plastic bag and pack out all poops. Don't do what some dog owners are guilty of by leaving the plastic bag alongside the trail—sanitation workers (or the Poop Fairy) will not come by to remove your dog's feces.
- **Use ID tags:** Make sure your dog has an identification tag with your current contact information, just in case he or she gets excited and wanders off.

Trail Etiquette and Safety

ETIQUETTE | The primary concern of trail etiquette is twofold: first, to make the hiking experience enjoyable for everyone and second, to protect the environment. These two goals can be easily accomplished by practicing the following guidelines:

- Leave no trace of your presence.
- In the wilds, dispose of waste properly. (Human feces should be buried six inches in the ground at least two hundred feet from water sources. Dog feces should be bagged and removed.)
- Stick to the trail—don't cut switchbacks, which causes erosion.
- Refrain from feeding or approaching wildlife.
- Pack out all litter. (Be a good Samaritan and pick up litter left behind by others.)
- Be quiet, inconspicuous, and respectful on the trail to avoid negatively affecting the experience of others.
- Refrain from collecting natural objects—leave them for others to enjoy.
- Yield the right of way to uphill hikers.
- Yield the right of way to large groups.
- Allow equestrians the right of way—step well off the trail on the downhill side.
- Allow mountain bikers the right of way, even though signs indicate the opposite. (It's a lot easier for a person on two legs to yield than expecting riders to get off their bike and move off the trail.)
- Report any major problems to land managers (trail washouts, trashed hunter's camps, illegal ATV damage, wildlife encounters, etc.).

SAFETY | Staying safe while hiking is of primary importance. Obviously, the requirements for a long hike into the backcountry will be greater than for those on a stroll through a city park.

- Be prepared.
- Pack plenty of water. When in the backcountry, purify all drinking water obtained from lakes and streams.
- Be cognizant of the weather—avoid exposed ridges and summits during the afternoon when thunderstorms may be a threat.
- Use caution when hiking in areas of unstable footing—loose boulders, small pebbles, icy patches, and so on.
- Dress in layers, stay dry, eat plenty of high-energy snacks, and know the warning signs of hypothermia.
- Use common sense.
- In the backcountry, carry the ten essential systems:
  1. Navigation (map and compass)
  2. Sun protection (sunglasses and sunscreen)
  3. Insulation (extra clothing)
  4. Illumination (flashlight or head lamp with extra batteries)
  5. First-aid kit

6. Fire (waterproof matches, lighter, candle)
7. Repair kit and tools
8. Nutrition (extra food)
9. Hydration (extra water)
10. Emergency shelter
- Additional items that may be handy:
  1. Insect repellent
  2. Toilet paper and hand sanitizer
  3. Cell phone
  4. Trekking poles
  5. Camera
  6. Binoculars
  7. Trash bag

How to Use This Guide

The trips in this guide have been categorized into four chapters loosely based on subregions of the greater Carson City area. The first region includes trips along or near the valley floor. The second group is composed of trips above the valley floor in the foothills. The third chapter contains routes outside of town in the neighboring mountains of the Carson Range. Trips in and around Washoe Valley make up the fourth chapter. After a short introduction, each trip contains pertinent information listed within several important headings.

LEVEL | This entry identifies the type of outing—stroll, walk, or hike—and the three levels of skill necessary to safely and enjoyably handle the trip: novice, intermediate, and advanced.

Strolls are classified as essentially flat and short and demand virtually no navigational skills. The trails are either paved or on very well graded natural surfaces. Just about anyone should be able to enjoy these trips. These trips require little if any experience.

Walks will include some elevation change and are generally longer than strolls. Some navigation will be required to safely complete the route. Trail surfaces will be natural and typically well graded.

Hikes are longer, steeper, and more technically challenging than walks, and they require a higher degree of navigation as well. Hiking experience is absolutely essential.

TIME | The duration of a hike is listed here, based on the amount of time necessary for the average hiker to complete the trip. People in excellent condition should be able to make these trips in a shorter length of time, while less physically fit individuals will require more time than what is listed. Longer trips have been categorized into parts of a day rather than hours, which are more general evaluations and may also vary with one's level of physical fitness.

LENGTH | Accurate round-trip distances have been computed for each trip. Out and back trips start and end at the same trailhead. Shuttle trips start and end at different trailheads, requiring two vehicles or being dropped off and picked up at two different locations. Loop trips start and end at the same trailhead but avoid much if any backtracking. Lollipop loops also start and end at the same trailhead, but they have an out-and-back segment necessary to access the loop section.

ELEVATION | The amount of elevation gain and loss appears under this heading. The elevation of out-and-back trips is listed as a one-way figure. Shuttle, loop, and lollipop loop trips are noted as round-trip figures.

DIFFICULTY | Divided into easy, moderate, strenuous, and very strenuous, this listing denotes the level of physical effort required to complete a trip. Just about anyone who is ambulatory should be able to complete easy trips, while only people who are extremely physically fit should attempt very strenuous trips.

USERS | Under this heading are the types of groups allowed to use the trails. These groups include hikers, runners, trail runners, mountain bikers, cyclists, and equestrians. Also noted under this heading is if the trip is particularly kid friendly.

DOGS | Many people wish to include their dogs on trips. In some areas, dogs are not allowed; in others, they must be on a leash. The designation "OK" means that dogs are permitted off leash.

SEASON | This heading indicates the time of year when a trip is usually free of snow and is suitable for hiking. During winter, some trails listed as open all year may have brief periods when they are snow covered, depending on current conditions.

BEST TIME | Taking into account such variable factors as weather, water levels, seasonal wildflowers, or autumn color, this entry attempts to identify the time of year when a particular trip might be at its peak of enjoyment.

FACILITIES | Here is where you'll find a listing of any significant facilities near the trailhead.

MAP | Pertinent maps appear here, which may be hard-copy maps available from retailers or government agencies or maps that can be downloaded onto a computer or smartphone from land agency or organizational websites.

MANAGEMENT | Government or, on occasion, private entities charged with the oversight of recreational lands appear under this heading, complete with contact information in case there are questions or concerns.

HIGHLIGHTS I Appearing under this heading are short listings of the main attractions for each trip, identifying the reason or reasons why this trip is worth your time and effort.

LOWLIGHTS I In contrast to the previous entry, this heading points out any negative aspects that users should be aware of when contemplating a particular trip.

TIP I Helpful information particular to trips is listed under this category.

KID TIP I For families with children, this entry provides helpful information for enjoying the trip with youngsters or for determining its suitability.

TRAILHEAD I Following GPS coordinates for the start of the trail, accurate instructions are provided for driving a vehicle to trailheads.

TRAIL I Accurate and detailed trip descriptions are found here.

MILESTONES I This table lists the major and significant points along the route with numbers corresponding to the accompanying map.

Legend

●●●●●●●●●●●●●●	Featured Trail	580	Interstate Highway
------------	Secondary Trail	431	State Highway
~~	Stream	~~~~	200-foot contour
~~	Intermittent Stream	~~~~	40-foot contour
○	Spring	+++++++++	Railroad
⬛	Developed Campground	•—•—•—•	Powerline
⬛	Trailhead	————	Boundary
⬛	Parking	⚒	Mine
▲	Mountain	4	Trip Number
⬛	Ranger Station	1	Milestone Number
⬛	Visitor or Information Center	41653A	Forest Service Road
⬛	Picnic Area	◇	Rock Cairn
⬛	Restroom	•—•	Gate
■	Point of Interest	BUS 395	
1,140'	Elevation		
580	Interstate Highway	50	

GO GREEN | For those who wish to give back their appreciation of our precious local resources, suggested activities or organizations to support are featured under this heading with the pertinent contact information.

OPTIONS | The last entry is sort of a catchall of opportunities to add experiences to each trip. Sometimes this includes additional hikes or trail extensions in the immediate area. Other activities might be listed, such as picnic areas. Nearby attractions may also appear here, as well as places close by to grab a bite or a brew.

CHAPTER ONE

EAGLE VALLEY AND THE CARSON RIVER

Eagle Valley and the Carson River make up the prime geographical features of what is referred to as Carson City. Whereas many towns in the United States were typically built along the banks of major rivers, during settlement the plains along the Carson were reserved primarily for ranching and agriculture while the city grew up well to the west. Such a pattern eventually produced a modern-day boon for recreationists, as many of the old ranches have nowadays found their way into the hands of the public. The river corridor is not the only area available to outdoor enthusiasts in the valley. The distinctive bump southeast of downtown known as Prison Hill offers a number of trails suitable for a wide range of users. In addition, a handful of parks overseen by Carson City Parks, Recreation, and Open Space provide short and generally easy paths. Even the community's hospital, Carson Tahoe Regional Medical Center, gets into the act with a quartet of paths of their own. Sixteen different trips within Eagle Valley are featured in this chapter, offering something for just about everyone.

Riverview Park

Nestled in a lovely parcel of land on the west bank of the Carson River, Riverview Park offers recreationists a trio of short and easy walks through a varied environment. Beginning near the Korean War Veterans Memorial and historic structures from the early ranching days of the Pierini family, the Full Loop, North Loop, and South Loop trails traverse the 108-acre parkland through areas of upland sagebrush, lush wetlands, and a cottonwood-shaded stretch of the river. At 1.6 miles, the Full Loop grants access to the longest strip of riverbank, while the shorter 0.8-mile North Loop and 1.0-mile South Loop only briefly visit the river. These gently graded paths also offer the opportunity to see some of the abundant wildlife that frequent the river corridor and neighboring wetlands.

LEVEL	Walk, novice
LENGTH	Varies, 0.8 to 1.6 miles, loop
TIME	1/2 to 1 hour
ELEVATION	Negligible
USERS	Hikers, trail runners, bikers, equestrians
DOGS	OK (not allowed in wetland areas)
DIFFICULTY	Easy
SEASON	All year
BEST TIMES	Spring, fall
FACILITIES	Interpretive signs, Korean War Veterans Memorial, picnic tables and covered picnic area, restrooms, trash cans
MAP	Carson City: *Riverview Park / Mexican Ditch Trail System* (web map at www.carson.org/home/showdocument?id =17489)
MANAGEMENT	Carson City Parks, Recreation, and Open Space at 775-887-2262, www.carson.org/government/departments-g-z/parks -recreation-open-space
HIGHLIGHTS	History, riparian area, river, wildlife
LOWLIGHTS	Hot in summer, exposed to sun

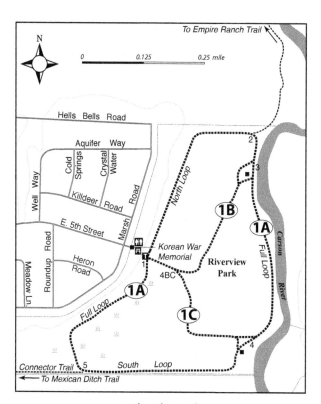

1. Riverview Park

TIP | Following winters of heavy precipitation, the river may flood areas of the park (as happened in 2017)—check with Carson City Parks, Recreation, and Open Space for current conditions.

KID TIP | As both waterfowl and land birds are plentiful in the Carson River environs, this trip might be a fine opportunity for school-age children to begin a bird checklist. The Nevada Division of Wildlife's (NDOW) website (www.ndow.org) has a checklist for birds of northwestern Nevada containing 289 species to be used in conjunction with the aid of a field guide to help identify the birds sighted. Additional online resources on the NDOW website are available to help customize an age-appropriate list with pertinent information and the space for children to draw pictures of the birds they see.

TRAILHEAD | 39°09.638′N, 119°42.627′W All three loops start from the Riverview Park trailhead. From downtown, head east away from South Carson Street on East 5th Street and drive 3 miles to the entrance into the parking lot for the Korean War Veterans Memorial and Riverview Parks, just past Marsh Road.

TRAIL | From the Riverview Park trailhead, head north on the Full Loop trail to the right of a low hill that obscures some of the housing development on Marsh Road, which lends a bit of wildness to the surroundings. Over the tops of the upland sagebrush vegetation are fine views to the north of McClellan Peak and the southern Virginia Range and to the east of a row of mature cottonwoods delineating the course of the Carson River back-dropped by the northern end of the Pine Nut Mountains beyond. Periodic park benches offer the opportunity to sit and enjoy the surroundings and the accompanying birdsong. Soon the trail bends east paralleling a barbed-wire fence on the way to the Carson River and an unmarked junction [2] with an old road providing a connection to the Empire Ranch Trail to the north.

Turn right at the junction and follow the west bank of the river upstream for a short way to the next junction [3] near a concrete-block utility building, where the North Loop veers southwest toward the trailhead. Continue ahead along the river beneath the shade of the old cottonwoods, as additional park benches allow more occasions to rest and watch the water glide downstream, as well as scan the area for waterfowl and a variety of mammals in search of a drink from the river. The gentle stroll along the riverbank eventually leads to the south end of the park and a Y junction [4] on the right with the South Loop near another concrete-block utility building.

Proceed ahead from the junction and wind around to the park boundary, where the trail turns west and follows a willow-lined ditch and a fence line with views of the distant Carson Range. Reach a three-way junction [5] with the Connector Trail to the Mexican Ditch Trail.

From the junction, the trail turns north and then northwest adjacent to lush wetlands, soon bending northeast and then north again on the return to the Riverview Park trailhead and the end of your loop. [1]

MILESTONES

1: Head north from trailhead; **2:** Veer right at Empire Ranch connector; **3:** Go straight at North Loop junctions; **4:** Go straight at South Loop junctions; **5:** Turn right at Connector Trail junction; **1:** Return to trailhead.

1B ▪ North Loop

TRAIL | From the Riverview Park trailhead, head north on the Full Loop trail to the right of a low hill that obscures some of the housing development on Marsh Road, which lends a bit of wildness to the surroundings. Over the tops of the upland sagebrush vegetation are fine views to the north of McClellan Peak and the southern Virginia Range and to the east of a row of mature cottonwoods delineating the course of the Carson River back-

A dog walker strolls through Riverview Park

dropped by the northern end of the Pine Nut Mountains beyond. Periodic park benches offer the opportunity to sit and enjoy the surroundings and the accompanying birdsong. Soon the trail bends east paralleling a barbed-wire fence on the way to the Carson River and an unmarked junction **[2]** with an old road providing a connection to the Empire Ranch Trail to the north.

Turn right at the junction and follow the west bank of the river upstream for a short way to the next junction **[3]** near a concrete-block utility building, where you veer southwest back toward the trailhead. Follow the North Loop through open sagebrush terrain in the center of the park to where the trail bends west and arrives at a junction **[4BC]** between the North and South Loops. Continue ahead, soon reaching the Riverview Park trailhead. **[1]**

MILESTONES

1: Head north from trailhead; **2:** Veer right at Empire Ranch connector; **3:** Turn right at North Loop junction; **4BC:** Go straight at South Loop junction; **1:** Return to trailhead.

1C ▪ South Loop

TRAIL ׀ From the trailhead, you head south on the combined course of the Full and South Loop trails to the right of a row of houses along Marsh Road and a patch of wetlands to the left. Very soon the trail bends southwest for a while before turning south again and shortly reaching a three-way junction **[5]** with the Connector Trail heading west to the Mexican Ditch Trail.

A muskrat near the river's edge

Turn left at the junction and follow the trail along a barbed-wire fence and a ditch toward the row of cottonwoods identifying the course of the Carson River. Nearing the river, the trail bends north and reaches the next junction [4] near a concrete-block utility building.

Turn left (west) and proceed across the heart of Riverview Park through typical sagebrush scrub for a while before the trail turns north and comes to a junction [4BC] between the North and South Loops. Veer to the left here and follow the combined course of the two trails a short way back to the Riverview Park trailhead. [1]

> **REDWING BLACKBIRD** (*Agelaius phoeniceus*) One of the United States' most common birds, redwings are frequently seen amid the wetlands around the Carson River. The brilliant red shoulder patches on males make this songbird easy to identify. Aggressive in defending nesting territory, these birds will loudly protest the approach of human intruders and will often attack larger birds that pose a threat. Feeding primarily on insects, redwings find the wetlands an ideal source of food.

MILESTONES
1: Head south from trailhead; 5: Turn left at Connector Trail junction; 4: Turn left at South Loop junction; 4BC: Turn left at North Loop junction; 1: Return to trailhead.

Red-winged Blackbird

GO GREEN ׀ A branch of the Carson City Historical Society, the Foundation for the Betterment of Carson City Parks and Recreation (The Park Foundation) is an independent, nonprofit organization working with government, community groups, and like-minded organizations to support and enhance the area's parks. For more information, consult their website at www.cchistorical.org/parkfoundation2.htm.

OPTIONS ׀ Those interested in extending their trips can easily do so by connecting to the Mexican Ditch Trail (Trips 2–3) to the west or the Empire Ranch Trail (Trip 6) to the north.

Mexican Ditch Trail North

A pleasantly graded route on natural and man-made surfaces connects Riverview Park to Moffat Open Space via a section of the Mexican Ditch Trail on the east side of Carson City near the Carson River. Along the way, travelers will experience a stretch of wetlands and the lazily flowing waters of the ditch at the very edge of suburbia.

LEVEL	Walk, novice
LENGTH	3.0 miles, out and back (1.5 miles with shuttle option)
TIME	1 hour
ELEVATION	Negligible
USERS	Hikers, runners, bikers, equestrians
DOGS	OK
DIFFICULTY	Easy
SEASON	All year
BEST TIMES	Spring, fall
FACILITIES	Picnic tables and covered picnic area, restrooms, trash cans
MAP	Carson City: *Riverview Park / Mexican Ditch Trail System* (web map at www.carson.org/home/showdocument?id =17489)
MANAGEMENT	Carson City Parks, Recreation, and Open Space at 775-887-2262, www.carson.org/government/departments-g-z/parks -recreation-open-space
HIGHLIGHTS	Ditch, history, wetlands, wildlife
LOWLIGHTS	Traffic crossings, exposed to sun—hot in summer

TIP | Although a fairly short hike by most standards, people with sensitive skin should lather up with sunscreen, as there is a definite lack of shade along the whole route.

KID TIP | This relatively short hike should be fine for school-age children, but very young ones should be constantly supervised along the unfenced ditch. A picnic lunch at Riverview Park would provide a fine reward at the end of the trip.

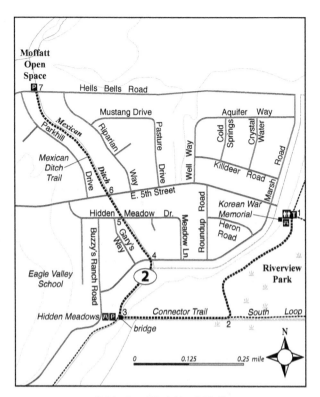

2. Mexican Ditch North Trail

TRAILHEAD | 39°09.440′N, 119°43.064′W From South Carson Street in downtown, head east on East 5th Street and drive 3 miles to the entrance into the parking lot for the Korean War Veterans Memorial and Riverview Parks, just past Marsh Road.

For the shuttle option, the ending trailhead at the south parking area for Moffatt Open Space is on the north side of Hells Bells Road near the intersection with Parkhill Drive. 39°09.638′N, 119°42.627′W

TRAIL | Head south on the wide track of an old road, soon trading the developed area of the park for a row of houses along Marsh Road sitting to the west of the trail. On the opposite side are lush wetlands filled with plants and birdsong. Eventually the trail bends away from the houses and leads shortly to an unmarked junction **[2]** with the Connector Trail at 0.3 mile. Near the junction is a park bench shaded by a Russian olive tree.

Turn right and follow the Connector Trail west along an irrigation ditch at the boundary between the end of the park and a pasture to the south. At 0.6 mile from the trailhead, you make a very brief ascent up a low hill, cross

View of the hills from the Mexican Ditch Trail

a bridge over the Mexican Ditch, and immediately reach a junction [3] with the Mexican Ditch Trail near the Hidden Meadows trailhead.

Bend to the right and proceed north on the ditch trail, which closely parallels the Mexican Ditch downstream. Sandwiched between houses on the left and the ditch to the right, you follow the gently graded path to a crosswalk at Marsh Road. [4] Pick up the trail again on the far side and proceed shortly to the next crosswalks at Hidden Meadow Drive [5] and East 5th Street. [6]

Continue to follow the ditch, which is lined with a mixture of sagebrush and willows, to the end of the Mexican Ditch Trail at Hells Bells Road. [7] On the far side of the pavement is a parking area for Moffatt Open Space.

BLACK-BILLED MAGPIE (*Pica hudsonia*) Members of the crow family, black-billed magpies are common residents of the Carson Valley and are frequently seen along the river corridor. Easily identified by an abnormally long tail, black head, and white belly, they also sport iridescent green, blue, and violet colors on wings and tail. Typically living up to six years, magpies generally mate for life.

MILESTONES

1: Head south on South Loop Trail; **2:** Turn right onto Connector Trail; **3:** Cross bridge and turn right at Mexican Ditch Trail; **4:** Cross Marsh Road;

Black-billed Magpie

5: Cross Hidden Meadow Drive; **6:** Cross East 5th Street; **7:** End at Moffatt Open Space parking area; **1:** Return to Riverview Park trailhead.

GO GREEN | Since 1998, the Nevada Land Trust has been instrumental in preserving and protecting open space and sensitive lands in Nevada. To learn more about their mission or to get involved in their work, visit their website at www.nevadalandtrust.org.

OPTIONS | Rather than simply returning the way you came to Riverview Park, an alternate route follows Hells Bells Road east to Riparian Way, south to East 5th Street, and then east back to the trailhead.

By leaving a second vehicle at the Moffatt Open Space parking area at Hells Bells Road, you could do a 1.5-mile shuttle trip instead of the out-and-back trip as described.

Paths in Riverview Park and Moffatt Open Space offer plenty of trip extensions for those who may be interested.

Mexican Ditch Trail South

Following the placement of two bridges over the Mexican Ditch in 2009, this section of the Mexican Ditch Trail provides a continuous link between Silver Saddle Ranch and Carson City's system of metro trails. This route between the Hidden Meadows trailhead and the entrance road to Silver Saddle Ranch is a 1.5-mile, one-way jaunt that follows the ditch upstream past pasture-land, ranches, and homes, offering nice scenery between Prison Hill to the southwest and the Pine Nut Mountains foothills to the east.

LEVEL	Walk, novice
LENGTH	3.0 miles, out and back (1.5 miles with shuttle option)
TIME	1 hour
ELEVATION	Negligible
USERS	Hikers, runners, bikers, equestrians
DOGS	OK
DIFFICULTY	Easy
SEASON	All year
BEST TIMES	Spring, fall
FACILITIES	Picnic tables, trash cans
MAP	Carson City: *Riverview Park / Mexican Ditch Trail System* (www.carson.org/home/showdocument?id=17489)
MANAGEMENT	Carson City Parks, Recreation, and Open Space at 775-887-2262, www.carson.org/government/departments-g-z/parks-recreation-open-space
HIGHLIGHTS	Ditch, wetlands, wildlife
LOWLIGHTS	Exposed to sun—hot in summer

TIP | Although a fairly short hike by most standards, people with sensitive skin should lather up with sunscreen, as there is a definite lack of shade along the whole route.

KID TIP | This relatively short hike should be fine for school-age children, but very young ones should be constantly supervised along the unfenced ditch. Kids should find the farm animals at the ranches near the midpoint a fascinating diversion.

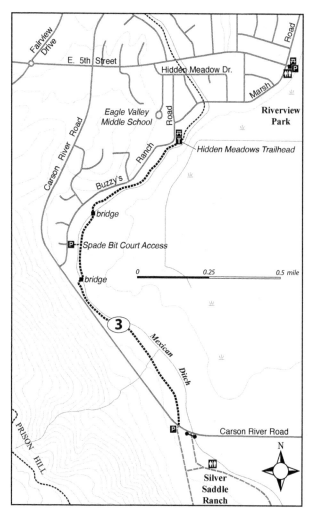

3. Mexican Ditch South Trail

TRAILHEAD | 39°09.440′N, 119°43.064′W From downtown, head east away from South Carson Street on East 5th Street and drive 2.4 miles to a right-hand turn onto Hidden Meadow Drive. Pass by the entrance to Eagle Valley Middle School and immediately turn right at Buzzys Ranch Road and then continue another 0.2 mile to the entrance to the parking area for the Hidden Meadows trailhead.

TRAIL | Turn south from the trailhead area and follow the Mexican Ditch lined with willows, wild rose, and sagebrush. To the right, you pass by the fenced backyards of homes along Buzzys Ranch Road, while on the left

The Mexican Ditch with Slide Mountain in the distance

are the bucolic pasturelands of a cattle ranch. Across the open ranchlands are views of the cottonwoods lining the Carson River and the Pine Nut Mountains foothills. About 0.5 mile into the journey, the trail crosses the ditch on a modern, steel-railed bridge built in 2009 and then follows the east bank past more homes and views across the pasture. Soon you reach a junction [2] with an access path on the right from the intersection of Buzzys Ranch Road and Spade Bit Court.

Continue ahead from the junction, as the trail merges with a dirt road serving the nearby ranch property. Pass by some ranch buildings and corrals on the way to a second bridge with a commemorative plaque thanking contributors for the span connecting the north and south sections of the trail. The road follows the course of the Mexican Ditch close to Carson River Road for a short stretch before veering to pass behind several home parcels. Beyond the last of these properties, you proceed generally south for a little while to where the ditch crosses below Carson River Road at the end of the route. [3] From there, retrace your steps to the Hidden Meadows trailhead. [1]

MILESTONES

1: Start at trailhead; 2: Go straight at junction; 3: End at Carson River Road; 1: Return to trailhead.

Western Fence Lizard

WESTERN FENCE LIZARD (*Sceloporus occidentalis*) A hike in the valleys of western Nevada without seeing one of these common reptiles is a rare experience. Dark brown, gray, or black on top, their blue undersides have led to the designation of "blue belly." The 2.5"- to 3.5"-long lizards are most easily seen on rock outcrops, sunning themselves or performing push-ups.

GO GREEN | Muscle Powered is the preeminent organization for building and maintaining trails in Carson City. Established in 1999, the group has been an unparalleled advocate for biking and hiking trails in the area. With the relatively recent placement of the two bridges across the Mexican Ditch in 2009, a lengthy connection has been established from the trail systems at

Silver Saddle Ranch and Prison Hill to the bike trail system in the middle of town. Along with trail building and maintenance, education, and advocacy, the nonprofit group hosts events and cleanup projects. You can become a member and support the work at www.musclepowered.org.

OPTIONS | Extending the trip is straightforward by connecting to the trail system at Silver Saddle Ranch (see Trips 14–16).

4 | Moffatt Open Space

A nearly eighteen-acre parcel of land lies on the east side of the city containing a stretch of Lower Kings Canyon Creek with accompanying riparian vegetation, a section of the Mexican Ditch, and an undeveloped pocket of land filled primarily with sagebrush and lesser amounts of ephedra, horsebrush, native grasses, and rabbitbrush. A paved bike path and a short interpretive loop provide short and easy access to the north part of the park, while a primitive tract of land to the south has many social trails.

LEVEL	Walk, novice
LENGTH	0.7 mile, out and back
TIME	1/2 hour
ELEVATION	Minimal
USERS	Hikers, runners, bikers
DOGS	OK
DIFFICULTY	Easy
SEASON	All year
BEST TIMES	Spring, fall
FACILITIES	Park benches, trash cans
MAP	Carson City: *Carson City Multi-Use Routes Map*, 4th ed.
MANAGEMENT	Carson City Parks, Recreation, and Open Space at 775-887-2262, www.carson.org/government/departments-g-z/parks-recreation-open-space
HIGHLIGHTS	Creek, ditch, interpretive signs, views
LOWLIGHTS	Exposed to sun—hot in summer

TIP | A pair of Girl Scouts from Troop 475 helped create the interpretive loop on top of the knoll in 2009. A plaque near the beginning provides interesting facts about the area keyed to numbered posts. Over time, the condition of the trail has deteriorated and could use some TLC.

KID TIP | The short interpretive trail offers an opportunity to engage children with the geography, geology, vegetation, and history of the surrounding area by utilizing the plaque and numbered posts positioned around the loop.

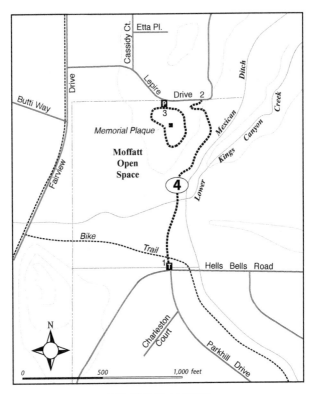

4. Moffatt Open Space

TRAILHEAD | 39°09.881'N, 119°43.304'W The south parking area for Moffatt Open Space is on the north side of Hells Bells Road near the intersection with Parkhill Drive. From South Carson Street, head east on East 5th Street for 2.2 miles and turn left onto Hells Bells Road. Continue another 0.3 mile to the intersection of Parkhill Drive and turn into the dirt parking area on the north side of the road.

The north trailhead is located on Lepire Drive, 0.1 mile east of Fairview Drive. 39°10.031'N, 119°43.322'W

TRAIL | From the parking area, a paved bike trail heads north, roughly paralleling a section of the Mexican Ditch to your right, soon arriving at a culvert carrying the waters of Lower Kings Canyon Creek, where a lush patch of wetlands, filled with cattails, rushes, and sedges, borders the stream. From there, the path climbs stiffly but briefly with the aid of a switchback up to the shoulder of Lepire Drive. [2] A short walk west along the road leads to the upper, north trailhead parking area. [3]

Follow the interpretive trail to a shade structure and then up a set of stairs to the top of the knoll and an impressive 360-degree vista. Nearby is

Lichen on the rocks in Moffatt Open Space

Moffatt Open Space Guide

a memorial plaque dedicated to the Moffatt family, who donated the surrounding lands. Also on top of the knoll is another plaque detailing information keyed to numbered posts positioned around the short interpretive loop. At the completion of the loop, retrace your steps to the south trailhead. [1]

WILLIAM H. MOFFATT (1875–1963) William Moffatt acquired a great deal of rangeland across northern Nevada in the 1920s. He also established the Union Land and Cattle Company and the Union Wool Company. He sold the land that would become Moffatt Open Space to the city as part of the first acquisition of the Open Space Division; the parcel was dedicated in 2002.

MILESTONES

1: Start at south trailhead; **2:** Turn left at Lepire Drive; **3:** Reach north trailhead and follow interpretive trail loop; **1:** Return to trailhead.

GO GREEN | Nevada Recreation and Park Society is a statewide nonprofit organization dedicated to training and developing professionals involved in parks, open space, and recreation. For more information, visit their website at www.nrps.org/.

OPTIONS | A number of bike paths and trails connect to the south trailhead to provide many opportunities for further wanderings. Also, the undeveloped portion of the open space to the south is crisscrossed with use trails ripe for further exploration.

Linear Park Trail

The Linear Park Trail is a multi-use, paved path heading east from Governors Field to the south Moffatt Open Space trailhead on Hells Bells Road, providing a straightforward connection to the Mexican Ditch Trail network. With multiple access points, trips of varying lengths can easily be created to fit the schedule and desires of walkers and bikers.

LEVEL	Walk, novice
LENGTH	6.0 miles, out and back (3.0 miles with shuttle option)
TIME	1-1/2 hours
ELEVATION	Negligible
USERS	Hikers, runners, bikers
DOGS	OK
DIFFICULTY	Easy
SEASON	All year
BEST TIMES	Spring, fall
FACILITIES	Ball fields, park benches, picnic tables, playground, restrooms
MAP	Carson City: *Carson City Multi-Use Routes Map*, 4th ed.
MANAGEMENT	Carson City Parks, Recreation, and Open Space at 775-887-2262, www.carson.org/government/departments-g-z/parks-recreation-open-space
HIGHLIGHTS	Paved path
LOWLIGHTS	Exposed to sun—hot in summer, freeway noise

TIP | Water is available at Governors Field but will be hard to come by farther along the trail, so pack a full container before setting out. Since shade is also at a premium, sunscreen should be applied to any exposed skin and reapplied as necessary.

KID TIP | The paved, dedicated path is a fine way to get young kids out on their bikes for a leisurely ride. However, there are several crossings of busy streets at South Saliman Road, Airport Road, and the roundabout at East 5th Street and Fairview Drive on the way to Moffatt Open Space if you plan to go the full distance.

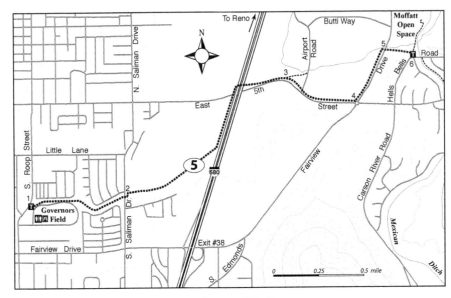

5. Linear Park Trail

TRAILHEAD | 39°09.213′N, 119°45.679′W From South Carson Street, head east on Fairview Drive to a left-hand turn onto South Roop Street. Go north for two blocks and turn right onto Evalyn Drive. The parking lot closest to the start of the paved bike path is on the north side of Governors Field.

For the shuttle option, the south parking area for Moffatt Open Space is on the north side of Hells Bells Road near the intersection with Parkhill Drive. From South Carson Street, head east on East 5th Street for 2.2 miles and turn left onto Hells Bells Road. Continue another 0.3 mile to the intersection of Parkhill Drive and turn into the dirt parking area on the north side of the road. 39°09.881′N, 119°43.304′W

TRAIL | From the parking lot, access the paved bike trail via a short walkway north of a crosswalk on Evalyn Drive. From there, head east alongside a ditch with accompanying riparian foliage. Continue past Governors Field, as the ditch bends and travels northeast along the fenced backyards of houses along Canvasback Drive. Proceed to a crosswalk at South Saliman Drive [2].

Once across the street, follow the paved path past some interpretive signs and across a bridge over the ditch. Heading east again, continue on the north side of the ditch past Fremont Elementary School to a parcel of natural, undeveloped land on the way toward the west side of the freeway. Here the path turns north-northeast and follows the edge of the noisy interstate for a while. After passing beneath the East 5th Street overpass, the

The Linear Park Trail attracts a wide range of users

route bends east and travels below the freeway to follow the north side of East 5th Street along another strip of undeveloped land to a Y junction. [3]

Veer right at the junction and soon encounter a crosswalk at Airport Road. Follow the route along East 5th Street past the sewage treatment plant to the roundabout [4] at the intersection with Fairview Drive.

Bend to the left at the roundabout and proceed northeast along Fairview Drive to where the path crosses Fairview Drive [5] and travels east along the ditch again to the Moffat Open Space parking area. [6]

MILESTONES
1: Start at trailhead; 2: Cross South Saliman Drive; 3: Veer right at junction; 4: Turn left at roundabout; 5: Turn right and cross Fairview Drive; 6: End at Moffatt Open Space parking area; 1: Return to trailhead.

> **MALLARDS** (*Anas platyrhynchos*) Along with Canadian geese, mallards are the most common waterfowl in the waterways of Eagle Valley. Males are easily identified by their iridescent-green heads, bright yellow bills, gray bodies, and black tails. The less colorful females have mostly brown bodies. These ubiquitous birds are found throughout North America. Humans should avoid the common practice of feeding bread to wild ducks, as doing so could inadvertently lead to malnutrition, overcrowding, pollution, loss of natural behavior, and susceptibility to diseases.

Mallards in flight

GO GREEN | The Lahontan Audubon Society is dedicated to preserving and protecting wildlife habitat in northern Nevada. You can learn more about their mission, programs, and activities at their website, www.nevadaaudubon.org.

OPTIONS | The Linear Park Trail provides connections to the short trails in Moffatt Open Space and the longer options along the Mexican Ditch Trail, which also connects to the trail networks in Riverview Park, Silver Saddle Park, and Prison Hill.

Empire Ranch Trail

The Empire Ranch Trail follows a peaceful stretch of the Carson River through a thin ribbon of natural area followed by a meandering course alongside the river adjacent to the manicured surroundings of the Empire Ranch Golf Course. Although he probably didn't actually say so, if you agree with the quote attributed to Mark Twain that golf is a "good walk spoiled," you should enjoy this nearly three-mile route around the fringe of one of Carson City's golf courses. The trailhead at Morgan Mill Park is where non-motorized boaters put in for the downstream float along the Carson River Aquatic Trail, but two-legged travelers head in the opposite upstream direction. Mature cottonwoods provide intermittent shade along the part of the route that follows the river until the trail bends away to traverse the southern edge of the golf course and then curves north to the terminus at the Empire trailhead. The area offers good opportunities to see wildlife through the river corridor and fine views of the surrounding hills and mountains.

Note: As of late 2019, the stretch of trail between Morgan Mill and Riverview Park along the Carson River was closed due to the river undercutting the narrow strip of land owned by the city between the river and the golf course. Carson City was working on a feasible solution to the dilemma, but hikers should contact Carson City Parks, Recreation, and Open Space to check on current conditions.

LEVEL	Walk, intermediate
LENGTH	6.0 miles, out and back (3.0 miles with shuttle option)
TIME	3 hours
ELEVATION	Negligible
USERS	Hikers, trail runners, mountain bikers, equestrians
DOGS	OK
DIFFICULTY	Moderate
SEASON	All year
BEST TIMES	Spring, fall
FACILITIES	Boat launch, park benches, picnic tables, portable toilets, trash cans
MAP	Carson City: *Carson City Multi-Use Routes Map*, 4th ed.

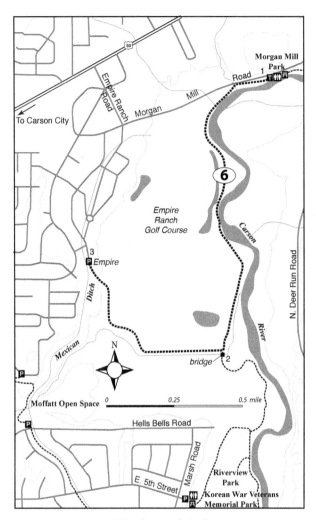

6. Empire Ranch Trail

MANAGEMENT	Carson City Parks, Recreation, and Open Space at 775-887-2262, www.carson.org/government/departments-g-z/parks-recreation-open-space
HIGHLIGHTS	Riparian zone, river, scenery, wildlife
LOWLIGHTS	Exposed to sun—hot in summer

TIP | Morgan Mill Park is open from dawn to dusk. Although there is intermittent shade from cottonwoods along the river, the rest of the route is exposed to the sun. Walk here in the morning or early evening if you plan to hike this

Kayakers floating the Carson River along the Empire Ranch Trail

trail in the summer months. Carson City recommends catch-and-release fishing only, due to mercury levels.

KID TIP | The essentially level trail is a fine place to bring the kids for exploring the riparian zone along the Carson River, but the close proximity to the water means adults will need to continuously supervise small children.

TRAILHEAD | 39°10.942′N, 119°42.349′W From North Carson Street, take East Williams Street (US 50) for 2.9 miles to a right-hand turn at Empire Ranch Road. After 0.2 mile, turn left onto Morgan Mill Road and drive another 0.5 mile to the entrance into Morgan Mill Park at a sign marked "Morgan Mill Road River Access Area."

For the shuttle option, the Empire trailhead is at the end of Empire Ranch Road, 0.8 mile south of US 50. 39°10.370′N, 119°43.038′W

TRAIL | Pick up the trail at the west edge of the parking lot near the boat launch, and immediately pass a Carson Trail historical marker for the Johnson Cutoff, where a nearby park bench provides an enticement to watch the river glide by while you sit and enjoy the scenery. The natural setting on the initial stretch of trail soon gives way to the park-like surroundings of the Empire Ranch Golf Course. The setting is quite pleasant, with the cottonwood-lined river on your left and excellent views over the emerald fairways of the distant Carson Range across the valley to your right. Continue down the course of a dirt road along a fence line dividing the riparian zone of the river and the golf course. Shade from intermittent groves of cottonwoods offers a nice break from the often intense sun, as you proceed south to a three-way junction, 1.2 miles from the trailhead. [2]

Directly ahead at the junction is a stout, steel-and-wood bridge spanning an irrigation ditch and a connector heading south to the trail system in River-view Park. However, you turn right and head west toward the Carson Range along the irrigation ditch and the southern fringe of the golf course. Follow a gravel road to the far edge of the golf course, where a dirt road winds around to the north. Eventually, you draw alongside the Mexican Ditch, where a melody of birdsong usually emanates from the riparian zone along this waterway. The road crosses over the ditch, passes by a utility building, and then makes a brief climb to a closed steel gate and the Empire trailhead [3] at the end of Empire Ranch Road. With shuttle arrangements, your trip is over. Otherwise, retrace your steps to the Morgan Mill trailhead. [1]

Morgan Mill When access to water from the Carson River was made easier by the completion of the Virginia & Truckee Railroad in 1869, eight stamp mills for processing ore were built in the canyon between Carson City and Moundhouse, including Morgan Mill. During the 1870s and 1880s, the canyon was a bustle of industrial activity brought on by the mills and associated infrastructure. In the milling process, vast quantities of mercury were used to separate gold and silver from the rock, more than 14 million pounds of which ended up in the Carson River system (along with plenty of arsenic and lead). In 1990, the EPA designated the Carson River Mercury Superfund Site, which extends from Empire to the end of the river at Stillwater Wildlife Refuge. Due to this designation, anglers are advised by the city to engage in catch-and-release fishing only.

MILESTONES

1: Start at Morgan Mill trailhead; 2: Turn right at junction; 3: End at Empire trailhead; 1: Return to Morgan Mill trailhead.

GO GREEN | Muscle Powered is the preeminent organization for building and maintaining trails in Carson City. Established in 1999, the group has been an unparalleled advocate for biking and hiking trails in the area. Along with trail building and maintenance, education, and advocacy, the nonprofit group also hosts community events. They routinely sponsor trash mobs, cleanup projects that make a valuable contribution to the beautification of the greater Carson City area. You can become a member and support the work at www.musclepowered.org.

OPTIONS | From the junction [2] you could continue south and connect with the Riverview Park or Mexican Ditch trail systems.

Ambrose Carson River Natural Area

Nestled into a strip of undeveloped land on the east bank of the Carson River, this 264-acre natural area is a relatively lightly used haven well suited for river lovers searching for an easy getaway from the city. Mature cottonwoods shade the riverbank and provide fine roosts for the abundance of birds that frequent the area. With a large tract of Bureau of Land Management (BLM) land to the east, plenty of four-legged critters find ways down to the water from time to time as well.

Two separate trails offer relatively short hikes for visitors, including a mile-plus-long romp along the river and an interpretive trail originally constructed by students from Carson High School. Time has not been kind to either of these paths, but both are distinct enough on the ground to be followed fairly easily, and plans are in the works for trail maintenance and improvements by the end of 2020. The interpretive trail has numbered posts corresponding to interesting tidbits about the area.

7A ▪ River Trail

LEVEL	Hike, intermediate
LENGTH	2.5 miles, out and back
TIME	1 hour
ELEVATION	+100'/–0'
USERS	Hikers, trail runners, mountain bikers, equestrians
DOGS	OK
DIFFICULTY	Easy
SEASON	All year
BEST TIMES	Spring, fall
FACILITIES	Portable toilet
MAP	Carson City: *Carson City Multi-Use Routes Map*, 4th ed.
MANAGEMENT	Carson City Parks, Recreation, and Open Space at 775-887-2262, www.carson.org/government/departments-g-z/parks-recreation-open-space

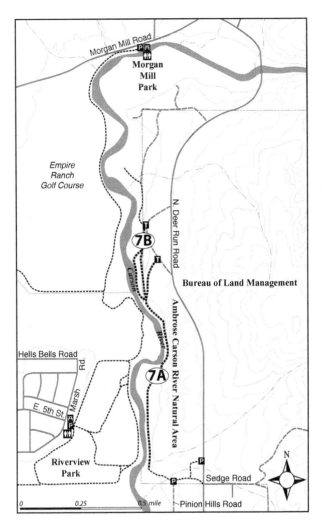

7. Ambrose Carson River Natural Area

HIGHLIGHTS Fishing, river, scenery, wildlife

LOWLIGHTS Indistinct trail network

TIP I A combination of factors—including flooding following the wet winter of 2016–2017, lack of use, and insufficient maintenance—has resulted in poor trail conditions throughout the natural area. Trails that appear on maps may be nonexistent on the ground. Carson City Parks, Recreation, and Open Space is hoping to rehabilitate the area in the near future.

KID TIP I Due to the concerns mentioned in the preceding section, the area might be deemed unsuitable by parents of small children until it receives

A tranquil stretch of the Carson River

some maintenance. Check with Carson City Parks, Recreation, and Open Space for current conditions.

TRAILHEAD | From North Carson Street in the center of town, follow East Williams Street (US 50) eastbound for 3.6 miles to a right-hand turn onto North Deer Run Road. Continue south another 1.75 miles to the second entrance for the Ambrose Natural Area on your right. Follow the gravel road about 500 feet to a small parking area near the start of the trail.

TRAIL | Other than a sign about the illegality of approaching wild horses, the trail was not marked in 2019. Head southwest on single-track tread through typical sagebrush scrub on a mild descent toward a grove of cottonwoods lining the Carson River. Reach the riverbank after 0.2 mile and turn upstream (south) on faintly defined tread. Around the half-mile mark, a steep cliff crowds the trail exceedingly close to the water's edge and may make the path impassable during high water, which may require an off-trail detour to circumvent. Beyond this potential obstacle, the plain widens out again, and easy travel quickly returns. Follow the winding course of the river to a flat shaded by cottonwoods, which may provide a fine spot for a picnic lunch or a rest stop. Proceed toward the far edge of the natural area, where the path ahead dies out and a more well-traveled trail angles slightly uphill to the left (east) and reaches the end of the graveled Pinion Hills Road. [2] From there, the path continues a short distance to the shoulder of North Deer Run Road [3] at the intersection of Sedge Road. Some maps indicate the presence of

Bald Eagle in flight

a loop trail paralleling North Deer Run Road back to the access road, which would provide a fine alternative to simply going back the way you came, but over time the path seems to have disappeared from the ground. Therefore, retrace your steps to the trailhead. [1]

BALD EAGLE (*Haliaeetus leucocephalus*) Although far from a common sight in the skies of western Nevada, bald eagles are occasionally seen along the Carson River, usually during the winter months. With increased concern focused on the river, the hope is that our national bird will become a more frequent visitor. The characteristic white, or "bald," head does not appear until the birds are about five years old. Despite a wingspan of six to seven feet that makes them appear to be quite large for birds, bald eagles only weigh between ten and fourteen pounds. When not nesting, they tend to be communal, with large groups roosting in tall trees.

MILESTONES

1: Start at trailhead; **2:** End of Pinion Hills Road; **3:** Shoulder of North Deer Run Road; **1:** Return to trailhead.

GO GREEN | The primitive conditions of the trail network in the Ambrose Carson River Natural Area begs for some attention from concerned citizens.

Volunteering with Muscle Powered would seem to be a logical step, and you can do so by visiting their website at www.musclepowered.org.

OPTIONS | Unlike the trail network on the opposite side of the river, there are no connections to trails beyond the Ambrose Carson River Natural Area. Also lacking are any nearby cafés or coffee shops for grabbing a post-hike treat. Perhaps your best bet is to pack a picnic lunch to enjoy next to the river.

7B ▪ Interpretive Trail

LEVEL	Walk, novice
LENGTH	0.5 miles, lollipop loop
TIME	1/4 hour
ELEVATION	Negligible
USERS	Hikers
DOGS	OK
DIFFICULTY	Easy
SEASON	All year
BEST TIMES	Spring, fall
FACILITIES	Portable toilet
MAP	Carson City: *Carson City Multi-Use Routes Map*, 4th ed.
MANAGEMENT	Carson City Parks, Recreation, and Open Space at 775-887-2262, www.carson.org/government/departments-g-z/parks-recreation-open-space
HIGHLIGHTS	Fishing, river, scenery, wildlife
LOWLIGHTS	Poorly maintained trail

TRAILHEAD | From North Carson Street in the center of town, follow East Williams Street (US 50) eastbound for 3.6 miles to a right-hand turn onto North Deer Run Road. Continue south another 1.5 miles to the first entrance for the Ambrose Carson River Natural Area on your right. Follow the gravel road about 1,000 feet to a parking area near the start of the trail.

TRAIL | Drop down from the parking area, and head south through sagebrush scrub to the start of the loop [2] near a signboard. Proceed down to the water's edge, and then return via the upper part of the trail to the loop junction. [2] From there, retrace your steps the short distance to the trailhead. [1]

Fulstone Wetlands

Designed as a buffer between the freeway and the Northridge subdivision, the eight-acre park known as Fulstone Wetlands offers hikers and riders a touch of natural landscape in the midst of the city. The park was dedicated in 2011 and has a 0.6-mile loop trail that wanders along and through a strip of wetlands filled with native and natural plants, including Apache plume, butterfly milkweed, daylilies, feather reed grass, and pinyon pine. Although such birds as redwing blackbirds, herons, red-tailed hawks, and mallards are the most common animals seen in this environment, coyotes and other mammals are infrequent visitors as well. A 63-foot-long mural (painted by a former student at Carson High) adorns the wall bordering the trail, adding an artistic element to the experience.

LEVEL	Stroll, novice
LENGTH	0.6 mile, loop
TIME	1/2 hour
ELEVATION	Negligible
USERS	Hikers, bicyclists, ADA accessible
DOGS	On leash
DIFFICULTY	Easy
SEASON	All year
BEST TIME	Spring
FACILITIES	Park benches
MAP	Carson City: *Carson City Multi-Use Routes Map*, 4th ed.
MANAGEMENT	Carson City Parks, Recreation, and Open Space at 775-887-2262, www.carson.org/government/departments-g-z/parks-recreation-open-space
HIGHLIGHTS	Wetlands, wildlife
LOWLIGHTS	Freeway noise, hot in summer, limited parking

TIP | As with most natural settings, your best opportunities to see wildlife typically occur just after sunrise or just before sunset.

KID TIP | The short and flat Fulstone Wetlands walking path make for a good option for young children, who should find the visiting birds to be quite

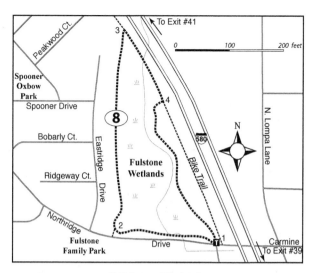

8. Fulstone Wetlands

entertaining. The Lahontan Audubon Society, based in Reno, offers field trips and classroom visits to help educate students about birds and conservation. Their website (www.nevadaaudubon.org) is a good place for more information about birds in our area.

TRAILHEAD | 39°10.750′N, 119°44.606′W Turn east from North Carson Street onto East Long Street, and travel 1.3 miles to a left-hand turn onto Russell Way. Continue 0.2 mile to the intersection of Northridge Drive. The start of the trailhead is on the north side of Northridge Drive, directly west of I-580. As there is no viable parking on Northridge, you should park your vehicle in the Boys and Girls Club parking lot across from the trailhead.

TRAIL | Start at the entrance to the wetlands near the Russell Way and Northridge Drive intersection and proceed westbound, paralleling the north side of Northridge Drive. Nearing the fenced subdivision, turn right (north) [2] onto the compacted surface of a natural trail, and proceed between the homes to the left and the wetlands area on your right. Continue to the far end of the wetlands, where you intersect the paved bike trail paralleling the freeway. [3] Turn right here and follow the bike trail a short way to where a natural-surface path veers to the right [4] and then wanders along through the drainage on the way back to the trailhead. [1]

> **GREAT BLUE HERON** (*Ardee herodias*) The great blue heron, often called a "crane," is the largest heron species in North America and has a distinctive appearance from its long legs, graceful neck, and dagger-like bill.

Hiker enjoying the trail through Fulstone Wetlands

Great Blue Heron and its young

Found in marshy areas and around riverbanks and lakes, these herons often stand motionless in their environments until a lightning-fast strike of their bills rewards them with a fish or other water-loving prey.

MILESTONES

1: Start at trailhead; **2:** Turn right; **3:** Turn right at bike trail junction; **4:** Turn right; **1:** Return to trailhead.

GO GREEN | A branch of the Carson City Historical Society, the Foundation for the Betterment of Carson City Parks and Recreation (The Park Foundation) is an independent, nonprofit organization working with government, community groups, and like-minded organizations to support and enhance the area's parks. For more information, consult their website at www.cchistorical.org/parkfoundation2.htm.

OPTIONS | The paved bike trail paralleling the freeway could provide opportunities for extending the trip northwest to College Parkway and points beyond.

Lone Mountain Trail

A raised bump of land in the middle of town, Lone Mountain separates a mixed commercial and residential area to the west and sprawling subdivision homes to the east, with a long, elevated slice of natural landscape offering wide-ranging views of the city and the surrounding hills. Other than a short climb away from the trailhead, the majority of the 0.5-mile dirt trail is a fairly easy romp across the spine of the north-south trending mountain.

LEVEL	Hike, novice
LENGTH	1.0 mile, out and back
TIME	1/2 hour
ELEVATION	+75′/–0′
USERS	Hikers, trail runners
DOGS	OK
DIFFICULTY	Moderate
SEASON	All year
BEST TIMES	Spring, fall
FACILITIES	None
MAP	Carson City: *Carson City Multi-Use Routes Map*, 4th ed.; US Geological Survey (USGS): *Carson City*
MANAGEMENT	Carson City Parks, Recreation, and Open Space at 775-887-2262, www.carson.org/government/departments-g-z/parks -recreation-open-space
HIGHLIGHTS	Views
LOWLIGHTS	Exposed to sun—hot in summer, homeless camps, trash

TIP | Although volunteers routinely pick up any trash that accumulates and authorities disperse the homeless from the area, if you witness either of these problems, contact the Parks Department immediately.

KID TIP | Lone Mountain is something of an interesting geologic feature in the midst of the city, which may prompt you to explore the Nevada Bureau of Mines website (www.nbmg.unr.edu) and follow links to science education and K-12 earth science educational resources for help in finding stimulating ways to engage kids with earth science.

9. Lone Mountain Trail

TRAILHEAD | 39°11.091′N, 119°45.536′W From North Carson Street, head east on Winnie Lane and turn left onto North Roop Street. Proceed north on Roop for 0.5 mile and turn right at Northridge Drive. After 0.1 mile, turn right again at the intersection with New Ridge Drive. The parking area is at the southwest corner of New Ridge and Northridge and is large enough for about a dozen vehicles.

TRAIL | The trail begins by angling away from the parking lot up a hillside and quickly switchbacking to the south. A steady ascent up the slope soon leads to the apex of the ridge and a wide-ranging view extending all the way south to the summits of Jobs and Freel Peaks and beyond to even more distant mountains. Closer at hand, you can see the Pine Nut Mountains rising to the east and Carson Range above the city's western border. Continue along the top of the ridge toward some utility poles and associated equipment before a very short but steep climb leads around the west side of a rocky knoll. Past this prominence, the single-track trail merges into a service road and proceeds toward the utility equipment perched on the next knoll. Pass the fenced utility equipment on the left and make a very short but steep

Wildflowers and rock formation on Lone Mountain

climb up to the high point [2] atop the next knoll, where a park bench offers a place to sit and enjoy the view. Immediately below are the grounds of the Lone Mountain Cemetery. When the time comes, retrace your steps to the trailhead. [1]

RUSSIAN THISTLE (TUMBLEWEED) (*Salsola tragus*) Almost as iconic as the cowboy himself is the sight of a tumbleweed rolling through

The ubiquitous tumbleweed

a deserted frontier town in a western movie. Ironically, this noxious plant is not native to North America. Transported here from the Russian steppes, the bush is now widely distributed throughout the American West. This troublesome annual weed has spiny stems when green. After the plant dies, the dried plant detaches from the root system to tumble away in the wind.

MILESTONES

1: Start at trailhead; **2:** High Point on Lone Mountain; **1:** Return to trailhead.

GO GREEN | Muscle Powered is the preeminent organization for building and maintaining trails in Carson City. Established in 1999, the group has been an unparalleled advocate for biking and hiking trails in the area. Along with trail building and maintenance, education, and advocacy, the nonprofit group also hosts community events. They routinely sponsor trash mobs, cleanup projects make a valuable contribution to the beautification of the greater Carson City area. You can become a member and support the work at www .musclepowered.org.

OPTIONS | Without any other trails in the immediate vicinity for extending your journey, you may want to consider grabbing some comfort food before or after the journey to Long Mountain. A five-minute drive away, the Cracker Box (402 East William St.) has been serving up tasty breakfasts and lunches in Carson City since 1980. Check out their website at www .thecrackerboxdiner.com, or visit their Facebook page.

TRIP

10 | # Carson Tahoe Regional Medical Campus

The award-winning medical campus of Carson Tahoe Health boasts four short trails suitable for grabbing some fresh air and enjoying the scenery. The first three trails are on the main campus and are flat and very well graded. The Wellness Mile encircles the property, following the sidewalk around Medical Parkway on a 1.15-mile loop. The Nature Trail is a natural surface trail bisecting the middle of the campus along the creek from Rose Canyon. The 0.25-mile Tranquility Trail, also known as the Serenity Stroll, makes a very brief loop around the Cancer Center through the pollinator garden and Bee Hotel. Aside from the interesting information about bees and their importance to the food chain, this extremely short path is perhaps the least interesting of the four trails to hikers. The newest addition to the trail system is the Foothill Trail, a natural hiking path branching from the pollinator garden on the north side of the property and climbing rigorously through Rose Canyon to a connection with the V & T Trail to Hobart Road. The trail is dedicated to Art Hannifin, who was an avid hiker, came up with the idea of this trail, and helped secure the easement that made it possible.

10A ▪ Wellness Mile

LEVEL	Stroll, novice
LENGTH	1.15 miles, loop
TIME	1/2 hour
ELEVATION	Negligible
USERS	Hikers, runners
DOGS	On leash
DIFFICULTY	Easy
SEASON	All year
BEST TIMES	Spring, fall
FACILITIES	None (restrooms and Starbucks in the hospital)
MAP	None
MANAGEMENT	Carson Tahoe Health at www.carsontahoe.com

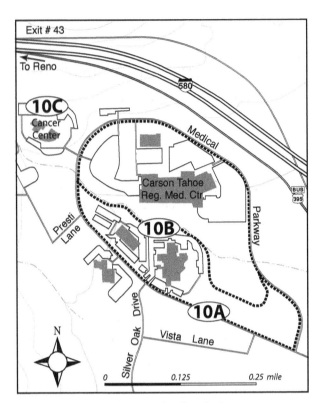

10. Carson Tahoe Regional Medical Campus

HIGHLIGHTS Scenery

LOWLIGHTS Hot in summer, exposed to sun, traffic noise

TIP | Early mornings, before traffic picks up at the hospital, offer perhaps the best time for using the paths on the campus.

KID TIP | The short, flat, and easy trails around the Carson Tahoe campus should be fine opportunities to get young kids interested in walking, especially if you reward them at the end with a beverage from Starbucks in the main hospital building.

TRAILHEAD | 39°12.124′N, 119°47.226′W From North Carson Street, turn west onto Medical Parkway and continue to one of the parking lots on the south or north sides of the creek draining Rose Canyon. Technically, the Wellness Mile begins at the sidewalk near the south parking lot and proceeds on a counterclockwise circuit along Medical Parkway. However, without shuttle arrangements or two vehicles, you'll have to walk the 0.15 mile between the north and south parking lots anyway, so it really makes little difference where you start.

TRAIL | The Wellness Mile follows the inner sidewalk around the length of Medical Parkway. Along the way, you can enjoy the pleasant urban surroundings of the hospital campus and the more distant views of the surrounding hills and mountains. Periodically placed signs offer mileposts to gauge your progress and helpful tips about better living.

10B ▪ Nature Trail

LEVEL	Stroll, novice
LENGTH	0.7 mile, out and back
TIME	1/2 hour
ELEVATION	Negligible
USERS	Hikers, runners
DOGS	On leash
DIFFICULTY	Easy
SEASON	All year
BEST TIMES	Spring, fall
FACILITIES	None (restrooms and Starbucks in the hospital)
MAP	None
MANAGEMENT	Carson Tahoe Health at www.carsontahoe.com
HIGHLIGHTS	Creek
LOWLIGHTS	Hot in summer, exposed to sun, traffic noise

TIP | Early mornings, before traffic picks up at the hospital, offer perhaps the best time for using the paths on the campus.

KID TIP | The short, flat, and easy trails around the Carson Tahoe campus should be fine opportunities to get young kids interested in walking, especially if you reward them at the end with a beverage from Starbucks in the main hospital building.

TRAILHEAD | 39°12.124′N, 119°47.226′W From North Carson Street, turn west onto Medical Parkway and continue to one of the parking lots on the south or north sides of the creek draining Rose Canyon. The trail starts from the inner sidewalk of Medical Parkway on the south side of the creek.

TRAIL | Follow the gently graded and wide path of a dirt roadbed alongside the creek draining Rose Canyon, which is lined with willows and other shrubs. Soon you reach a junction with a path on the left heading across a substantial wood-plank-and-steel bridge over the stream to a fenced garden with raised beds and then to the main hospital building (Starbucks, restrooms). Continue ahead, as the trail bends to the south and passes by some retention basins. Away from the lush vegetation along the creek, the trail is lined with typical sagebrush scrub. Soon the trail bends back toward the east, merges with a brief stretch of concrete, and then follows a dirt path

At the start of the Nature Trail

north to the end of the trail [2] at the shoulder of Medical Parkway. From there, retrace your steps to the trailhead, [1] or head either direction on the Wellness Mile back to the car.

10C ▪ Foothill Trail

LEVEL	Stroll, novice
LENGTH	2 miles, out and back
TIME	1 hour
ELEVATION	+275'/−275'
USERS	Hikers, runners, mountain bikers
DOGS	On leash
DIFFICULTY	Moderate
SEASON	All year
BEST TIMES	Spring, fall
FACILITIES	None (restrooms and Starbucks in the hospital)
MAP	None
MANAGEMENT	Carson Tahoe Health at www.carsontahoe.com; Carson City Parks, Recreation, and Open Space at 775-887-2262, www .carson.org/government/departments-g-z/parks-recreation -open-space
HIGHLIGHTS	Creek
LOWLIGHTS	Hot in summer, exposed to sun, traffic noise

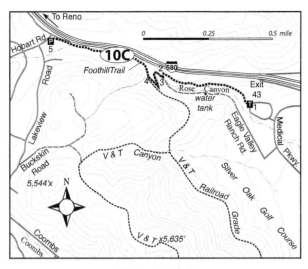

10C. Foothill Trail

TIP | When afternoon temperatures are forecasted to be hot, getting an early start would be a wise plan.

KID TIP | At 2 miles, out and back, this trip might be a good option for small children ready to hike under their own power. When the seasonal creek in Rose Canyon has water, the stream is a relatively safe playground for supervised small children.

TRAILHEAD | 39°12.243′N, 119°47.338′W From North Carson Street, turn west onto Medical Parkway and continue to the entrance into the Cancer Center property at the north end of the campus. Park your vehicle in the back lot near the garden and greenhouse.

TRAIL | Head away from the parking lot past the garden and greenhouse up a slope to the right of the willow- and cottonwood-lined stream draining Rose Canyon and to the left of the steep embankment below the I-580 freeway. Farther on, dense vegetation forces the trail farther up the hillside and along a section of old roadbed. Just beyond where you pass beneath a utility line, cross over a seasonal stream channel across the canyon from a pair of newer and older water tanks. A short, gentler stretch of trail leads across a grassy patch before the stiff climb resumes through sagebrush scrub to where the trail bends to the left and crosses the main stem of the creek [2] lined with riparian vegetation. Climb up the slope above the creek to merge with the utility road [3] servicing the water tanks below.

Follow the road upslope for a bit to a switchback and on to where you merge with the old V & T Railroad bed. [4] Follow the bed for a short while

Bee on flower

to the top of a small bluff above the freeway, where the old grade has disappeared in the wake of the more recent freeway construction. Here, newly built single-track trail slices across the steep hillside above the freeway on a steady upward traverse toward Hobart Road at the end of the trail. **[5]** From there, either retrace your steps a mile to the trailhead, or consider continuing your trip on a variety of extensions (see Options below)

MILESTONES

1: Start at trailhead; **2:** Cross creek; **3:** Right at service road; **4:** Right at V & T Railroad grade; **5:** End at Hobart Road; **1:** Return to trailhead.

BEE HOTEL/HABITAT AND POLLINATOR GARDEN The Foothill Garden located behind the Cancer Center near the trailhead has been producing fresh herbs and vegetables since 2017. A more recent addition to the area is the Bee Hotel/Habitat and Pollinator Garden, which offers habitat for leaf cutter bees, a nonaggressive species, to live and pollinate. The decline in bee populations and the importance of bees' role in the food chain has been well documented, and this project will enhance the sustainable production of organic produce in the hospital's Foothill and Creekside Gardens. For more information, visit Carson Tahoe's website at www.carsontahoe.com/garden.

GO GREEN | Muscle Powered is the preeminent organization for building and maintaining trails in Carson City. Established in 1999, the group has been an unparalleled advocate for biking and hiking trails in the area. Along with trail building and maintenance, education, and advocacy, the nonprofit group also hosts community events. They routinely sponsor trash mobs, cleanup projects that make a valuable contribution to the beautification of the greater Carson City area. You can become a member and support the work at www.musclepowered.org.

OPTIONS | Hikers, trail runners, and mountain bikers have a number of opportunities for extending their trips, as one of the prime motivations for building this trail was to complete a missing link in the network. Once at Hobart Road, recreationists can tie into the Marlette-Hobart backcountry system, including using the also newly built Secret Trail (Trip 49) down Vicee Canyon to create a shuttle or loop trip to Carson Tahoe Hospital. Other options include using either the V & T Railroad Grade (Trip 18) and V & T Ridgeline and Canyon (Trip 19) Trails for shuttle or loop trips.

11 | V & T Multi-Use Path

Located to the west of Western Nevada Community College is a paved, multi-use path that follows a stretch of the old alignment of the Virginia & Truckee Railroad. The north portion of the trail bisects developed lands to the east and an undeveloped tract of land to the west harboring numerous social trails. The nearly two-mile, out-and-back journey is a favorite among walkers, joggers, skaters, dog walkers, and workers from nearby businesses out for a lunchtime stroll.

LEVEL	Stroll, novice
LENGTH	1.8 miles, out and back
TIME	3/4 hour
ELEVATION	Negligible
USERS	Hikers, runners, bikers, equestrians
DOGS	OK
DIFFICULTY	Easy
SEASON	All year
BEST TIMES	Spring, fall
FACILITIES	None
MAP	Carson City: *Carson City Multi-Use Routes Map*, 4th ed.
MANAGEMENT	Carson City Parks, Recreation, and Open Space at 775-887-2262, www.carson.org/government/departments-g-z/parks-recreation-open-space
HIGHLIGHTS	Paved path, views
LOWLIGHTS	Hot in summer, exposed to sun

TIP | Summer users should start early in the day to beat the heat.

KID TIP | Plenty of small children find their way onto the V & T Multi-Use Path, either on foot, in a stroller, or snuggled into a kid carrier. As the trail is quite popular with a wide range of users, sometimes diligence is required to keep everyone safe.

TRAILHEAD | 39°11.160'N, 119°47.584'W From North Carson Street, turn west onto West College Parkway and drive 0.7 mile to a right-hand turn onto

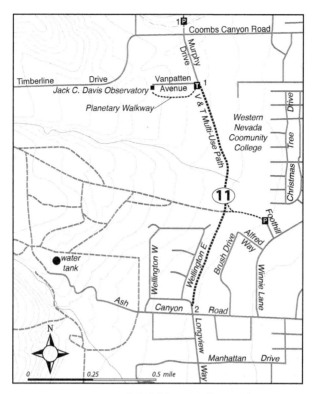

11. V & T Multi-Use Path

North Ormsby Boulevard. After 0.2 mile Ormsby turns west and becomes Coombs Canyon Road, which you follow another 0.5 mile to the intersection with Murphy Drive. Turn left and follow Murphy Drive 0.1 mile to the parking area immediately past Vanpatten Avenue.

TRAIL | Head away from the parking area on the wide, paved path at a very pleasant grade. On the left is the campus of Western Nevada Community College, while sagebrush scrub covers the open space on the opposite side. The open space is crisscrossed with numerous paths and old roads, but you're never in danger of wandering off the clearly obvious route of the V & T Multi-Use Path. Just beyond the college's ball fields, the path crosses Vicee Canyon Creek and continues the gently graded journey. Soon you encounter a large storm water retention basin sitting just off the trail to the east. At the far side of the basin and just before the fenced backyards of some subdivisions, a dirt trail on the left comes in from the Foothill Drive trailhead.

The remaining 0.3 mile proceeds between the backyards of houses behind a concrete wall on your right and an open fence line of houses to your left. Eventually you walk onto the sidewalk adjacent to Wellington South and soon reach the intersection with Ash Canyon Road. [2] Unless you have a vehicle waiting nearby, retrace your steps to the trailhead. [1]

MILESTONES

1: Start at trailhead; 2: Ash Canyon Road; 1: Return to trailhead.

VIRGINIA & TRUCKEE RAILROAD The V & T Railroad was born out of a need to transport ore from the Comstock Lode to quartz reduction mills alongside the Carson River. The company was organized in March 1868 with banks, mining companies, and financiers as major players. After a twenty-one-mile route between Carson City and Virginia City was surveyed, construction of a standard gauge rail line was completed in early 1870. About two and a half years later, a thirty-one-mile extension was constructed from Carson City through Franktown, Washoe City, and Steamboat Springs to a connection with the transcontinental railroad in Reno. The railroad was a huge economic boon for a couple of decades, attaining the distinction of being the most glamorous and wealthiest short line railroad in the world.

Hard times hit the mines early in the 1890s, and the railroad suffered as well until mining resurged early in the next century. A new V & T Railway Company was incorporated in 1905, and an extension was planned south from Carson City to the burgeoning grazing and agricultural district near Minden. This line produced steady revenues until a decline began when a highway was completed in the 1920s. Eventually unable to compete with the expansion of the highway system, the V & T's last official run was made on May 31, 1950.

Private investors began the process of restoring the V & T in the early 1970s, initiating a decades-long process of rebuilding the line and finding the necessary rolling stock. Along the way, local and state governments joined the process, and the Nevada Commission for the Reconstruction of the V & T Railway was created. For information about riding the train, visit the V & T website at www.vtrailway.com.

GO GREEN | Muscle Powered is the preeminent organization for building and maintaining trails in Carson City. Established in 1999, the group has been an unparalleled advocate for biking and hiking trails in the area. Along with trail building and maintenance, education, and advocacy, the nonprofit group also hosts community events. They routinely sponsor trash mobs, cleanup projects that make a valuable contribution to the beautification of the greater Carson City area. You can become a member and support the work at www.musclepowered.org.

OPTIONS | At the southern terminus of the V & T Multi-Use Path you can connect with the Carson City system of bike routes as delineated on the *Carson City Multi-Use Routes Map*.

Jack C. Davis Observatory
Planetary Walkway

0   500   1,000 feet

The Planetary Walkway at the Jack C. Davis Observatory on the west side of town is an informative walk with a slight touch of whimsy. Connecting the campus of Western Nevada College with the observatory, the quarter-mile-long path has twelve stops featuring details about the celestial bodies in our solar system, creating an entertaining and educational journey literally through the high desert and figuratively through the universe. Along with the pertinent scientific facts, each sandstone sculpture has a short dedication from donors to a beloved family member or friend, some providing the source of whimsy. Inmates from the Nevada State Prison created the sculptures, and volunteers helped with the installation and trail building, completing the project in time for the grand opening celebration on May 15, 2003. *Note: the very short trail heads downhill from the observatory grounds to the V & T Multi-Use Path trailhead near the corner of Vanpatten Avenue and Murphy Drive, so unless you have a vehicle waiting at the lower trailhead, you will have to climb back to the observatory.*

LEVEL	Walk, novice
LENGTH	0.5 mile, out and back
TIME	1/2 hour
ELEVATION	+0'/−100'
USERS	Hikers
DOGS	Not advised
DIFFICULTY	Moderate
SEASON	All year
BEST TIMES	Spring, fall
FACILITIES	Park benches, observatory
MAP	None
MANAGEMENT	Western Nevada College at www.wnc.edu
HIGHLIGHTS	Interpretive displays
LOWLIGHTS	Exposed to sun—hot in summer

TIP | The observatory is open on Saturday evenings throughout the year, from sundown to 11:00 P.M. Additional viewing opportunities of eclipses

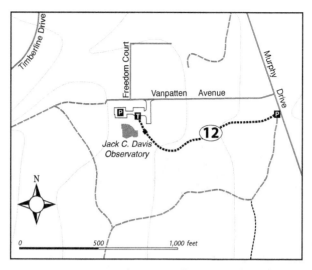

12. Planetary Walkway

and meteor showers may be available as scheduled (consult www.wnas
-astronomy.org/ for a calendar of events).

KID TIP | Plan an evening visit to the observatory for stargazing. Abundant
online resources are available for getting your youngsters interested in
astronomy.

UPPER TRAILHEAD | 39°11.156′N, 119°47.784′W From North Carson Street,
turn west onto West College Parkway and drive 0.7 mile to a right-hand
turn onto North Ormsby Boulevard. After 0.2 mile Ormsby turns west and
becomes Coombs Canyon Road, which you follow another 0.5 mile to the
intersection with Murphy Drive. Turn left and follow Murphy Dr. 0.1 mile to
a right-hand turn at Vanpatten Drive. Continue up Vanpatten to the entrance
into the Jack C. Davis Observatory parking lot on your left.

LOWER TRAILHEAD | 39°11.160′N, 119°47.584′W From North Carson Street,
turn west onto West College Parkway and drive 0.7 mile to a right-hand
turn onto North Ormsby Boulevard. After 0.2 mile Ormsby turns west and
becomes Coombs Canyon Road, which you follow another 0.5 mile to the
intersection with Murphy Drive. Turn left and follow Murphy Dr. 0.1 mile
to the parking area immediately past Vanpatten Avenue.

TRAIL | The trail begins near the southeast side of the parking lot and pro-
ceeds to a short bridge over a drainage channel near the edge of the developed part of the observatory grounds. Beyond the bridge, the wide gravel
path arcs around to the east and heads downhill through sagebrush scrub on

Mercury monument on the Planetary Walkway

the way to the V & T Multi-Use Path trailhead. [2] Along the way are sandstone sculptures with plaques for the following heavenly bodies arranged from closest to farthest from the Sun, which is the first monument: Mercury, Venus, Earth/Moon, Mars, Ceres, Jupiter, Saturn, Uranus, Neptune, Pluto, Quaoar. Without shuttle arrangements, you will have to walk back uphill to the upper trailhead. [1]

> **JACK C. DAVIS** (1925–2009) Davis was the founding president of Western Nevada Community College and served the institution from 1972 to 1983. While president, he helped establish satellite rural community college campuses in Fallon, Gardnerville, and Elko. As well as an academician, he was a student athlete in college and an official in varying capacities for local and worldwide sporting organizations.

MILESTONES
1: Start at observatory trailhead; **2:** End of trail at V & T Multi-Use Path trailhead; **1:** Return to observatory.

GO GREEN | The Western Nevada Astronomical Society was founded in 2002 by an observing group of amateur astronomers, who support the Jack C. Davis Observatory and the local astronomical community through educational programs, social functions, and service. Membership in the organization provides individuals and families with certain benefits. For more information, visit the website at www.wnas-astronomy.org.

OPTIONS ⎸ Extending your stroll on the V & T Multi-Use Path from the lower trailhead would be a straightforward affair.

Situated along the west side of Carson City, the Long Ranch Park pathways offer a convenient location for residents to get outside and stretch their legs. A number of interconnected walkways and paths provides easy access to the trail system from a variety of starting points. Riparian areas along both Kings Canyon and Ash Canyon Creeks certainly lend a more natural ambiance to the manicured area of Long Ranch Park at the start of the two loops. The short Inner Loop is a fine option for taking a short stroll, walking the dog, or helping a toddler perfect their gait, while the longer Open Space Loop allows users to get in a bit more exercise.

13A ▪ Inner Loop

LEVEL	Stroll, novice
LENGTH	0.6 mile, loop
TIME	1/4 hour
ELEVATION	Negligible
USERS	Hikers, cyclists
DOGS	On leash in developed area of park, off leash otherwise
DIFFICULTY	Easy
SEASON	All year
BEST TIMES	Spring, fall
FACILITIS	Horseshoe pits, park benches, playground, picnic tables and covered picnic area, trash cans, water for dogs
MAP	None
MANAGEMENT	Carson City Parks, Recreation, and Open Space at 775-887-2262, www.carson.org/government/departments-g-z/parks-recreation-open-space
HIGHLIGHTS	Creek
LOWLIGHTS	Hot in summer, exposed to sun

TIP ▏ The park is open from dawn to dusk. Bears and coyotes have been active in this area in the past.

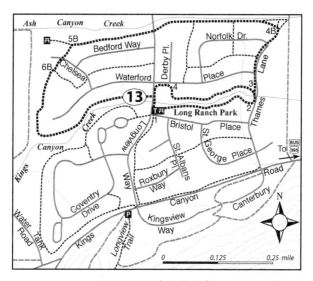

13. Long Ranch Park Trails

KID TIP | This easy trip through a city park should be a fine choice for young children, as the distance is short and the elevation change is unnoticeable. The usual flow of the creek is low enough to provide a safe space for youngsters to toss sticks into the water or look for bugs. The playground and picnic tables in the developed areas of the park can be good choices for play or a picnic lunch.

TRAILHEAD | 39°09.929'N, 119°47.549'W From North Carson Street, turn west onto West Musser Street and proceed for three blocks to a left-hand turn onto Division Street. After one block, turn right at West King Street and continue for 1.2 miles to Longview Way. Turn right at Longview and proceed 0.2 mile to the intersection of Bristol Way at the southwest corner of Longview Park. Park along the side of the street as space allows.

TRAIL | Begin the journey along the Inner Loop by following a concrete sidewalk past the picnic shade structure and playground through the manicured section of Long Ranch Park with Kings Canyon Creek to your left. Pass by a path on your right that heads south to Bristol Place and continue the downstream journey. Where the sidewalk meets the backyards of the houses along Bristol Place and Waterford Place, you enter a less-developed part of the park. Continue eastbound past another patch of lawn to the sidewalk along Thames Lane [2] and turn left.

As you walk north along Thames Lane, you cross Kings Canyon Creek and soon come to the path [3] that leads back upstream past more park benches toward the west end of Long Ranch Park. Nearing another patch

Kings Canyon Creek

of lawn beyond the end of the houses, the path bends to the north, passes a pair of picnic tables, and reaches the sidewalk along Waterford Place. [4] Turn left here, walk a short distance toward Longview Way, and then turn left again to return to the trailhead. [1]

MILESTONES

1: Start at trailhead; **2:** Turn left at Thames Lane; **3:** Turn left at sidewalk; **4:** Turn left at Waterford Place; **1:** Return to trailhead.

13B ▪ Long Ranch Estates Open Space Loop

LEVEL	Stroll, novice
LENGTH	1.9 miles, loop
TIME	1 hour
ELEVATION	Negligible
USERS	Hikers, cyclists
DOGS	On leash
DIFFICULTY	Easy
SEASON	All year
BEST TIMES	Spring, fall
FACILITIES	Park benches, playground, picnic tables and covered picnic area, trash cans
MAP	None

MANAGEMENT Carson City Parks, Recreation, and Open Space at 775-887-2262, www.carson.org/government/departments-g-z/parks-recreation-open-space

HIGHLIGHTS Creek

LOWLIGHTS Hot in summer, exposed to sun

TRAILHEAD | 39°09.929′N, 119°47.549′W From North Carson Street, turn west onto West Musser Street and proceed for three blocks to a left-hand turn onto Division Street. After one block, turn right at West King Street and continue for 1.2 miles to Longview Way. Turn right at Longview and proceed 0.2 mile to the intersection of Bristol Way at the southwest corner of Longview Park. Park along the side of the street as space allows.

TRAIL | Begin the journey along the Inner Loop by following a concrete sidewalk past the picnic shade structure and playground through the manicured section of Long Ranch Park with Kings Canyon Creek to your left. Pass by a path on your right that heads south to Bristol Place and continue the downstream journey. Where the sidewalk meets the backyards of the houses along Bristol Place and Waterford Place, you enter a less-developed part of the park. Continue eastbound past another patch of lawn to the sidewalk along Thames Lane [2] and turn left.

As you walk north along Thames Lane, you cross Kings Canyon Creek and soon come to the path [3] that leads back upstream past more park benches toward the west end of Long Ranch Park. Instead of following the sidewalk back to the trailhead as described in Trip 13A, go straight ahead at this junction and continue northbound along Thames Lane across Waterford Place and Norfolk Drive to a paved path between a couple of houses, which then makes a sweeping bend to the west [4B] and heads upstream along Ash Canyon Creek through an area of greenbelt. Go straight at a couple of junctions with paths on the left that head into the subdivision before reaching Longview Way. Carefully cross the street and pick up the resumption of asphalt path on the west side of Longview.

Continue up a paved path through a greenbelt along Ash Canyon Creek behind the fenced backyards of homes lining Bedford Way. Reach a three-way junction, [5B] where the right-hand path travels just a short distance to a paved turnaround with a picnic table. Veer left at the junction, cross Chelsea Place, and continue through a gap between a couple of houses to another junction [6B] with a path leading past some fenced backyards and around to a crossing of Chelsea Place. Go straight at this junction and stroll across a small pocket of undeveloped land to a three-way junction [7B] at the edge of the housing development. The path ahead accesses Waterford Place, but you turn right and wrap around between the backyards of the homes lining

Northern Flicker

the cul de sac to your left and an irrigation ditch to your right. Follow the path as it bends to the north and heads downstream along the west bank of Kings Canyon Creek. Proceed straight ahead where a side path leads over to Waterford Place, continue to Longview Way, use the crosswalk to access the sidewalk on the north side of Longview Way, and then turn right to walk the short distance to the trailhead at Long Ranch Park. [1]

> **NORTHERN FLICKER** (*Colaptes auratus*) The northern flicker seen in our area is a fairly large member of the woodpecker family, mostly brown in color with red under its wings and tail as seen in flight. Males also have a distinctive red strip behind their bills. Although a woodpecker, the northern flicker spends most of the time on the ground, hunting primarily for ants and other insects. They will also consume fruits and berries during autumn. Nests are found mostly in tree or post cavities.

1: Start at trailhead; **2:** Turn left at Thames Way; **3:** Go straight at sidewalk junction; **4B:** Curve west; **5B:** Turn left at junction; **6B:** Straight at junction; **1:** Return to trailhead.

GO GREEN | Muscle Powered is the preeminent organization for building and maintaining trails in Carson City. Established in 1999, the group has been an unparalleled advocate for biking and hiking trails in the area. Along with trail building and maintenance, education, and advocacy, the nonprofit group also hosts community events. They routinely sponsor trash mobs, cleanup projects that make a valuable contribution to the beautification of the greater Carson City area. You can become a member and support the work at www.musclepowered.org.

OPTIONS | Numerous connections offer the possibility of extending your trip in a variety of ways. A good way to plan out trip extensions is to view the area on Google maps.

Prison Hill Recreation Area

Rising above the surrounding terrain in the southeast corner of Carson City is a steep prominence known as Prison Hill. With a variety of routes incorporating sections of single-track trail and old roads, the north section of the 2,500-acre Prison Hill Recreation Area offers hikers, trail runners, mountain bikers, and equestrians diverse opportunities well suited for jaunts of varying lengths and difficulties, particularly in the spring and fall. The Sagebrush, Rabbitbrush, and Bitterbrush Loop is a 2-mile circuit around the north end of Prison Hill offering fine views to the west and east. The North Loop is about twice as long and requires a bit more elevation gain but also offers incomparable views of the Pine Nut Mountains and Carson Range on its tour around the hill. At 2.5 miles and only 200 feet of elevation gain, the West Loop is perhaps the easiest of the four routes described here, coursing across the lower elevations along the west side of the hill. Despite the lower elevation, the West Loop still offers fine views as well across Eagle Valley to the peaks of the Carson Range. The final entry of the four trips described here is a route up the west side of the mountain to the high point of Prison Hill. The stiff 1.25-mile climb to the summit will reward peak baggers with spectacular views of the surrounding terrain. *Note: proposed improvements to the Prison Hill network of trails may significantly alter the descriptions provided below in the near future, but they should dramatically improve the recreational experience for all users.*

14A ▪ Sagebrush, Rabbitbrush, and Bitterbrush Loop

LEVEL	Hike, intermediate
LENGTH	2 miles, loop
TIME	1 hour
ELEVATION	+600'/−600'
USERS	Hikers, mountain bikers, trail runners, equestrians
DOGS	OK
DIFFICULTY	Moderate
SEASON	All year

BEST TIMES	Spring, fall
FACILITIES	None
MAP	Carson City: *Prison Hill Recreation Area and Silver Saddle Ranch* (https://www.carson.org/home/showdocument?id =38830) *Note: trail is not accurately shown on map.*
MANAGEMENT	Carson City Parks, Recreation, and Open Space at 775-887-2262, www.carson.org/government/departments-g-z/parks-recreation-open-space
HIGHLIGHTS	Views
LOWLIGHTS	Exposed to sun—hot in summer

TIP | Recent improvements, including upgraded trailhead and a new alignment, make this trip much more desirable than the previous iteration.

KID TIP | The three stacked loops above the trailhead allow parents the opportunity to customize the length of a hike to fit the abilities of their offspring. Without shade, hikes on Prison Hill necessitate plenty of sun protection.

TRAILHEAD | 39°09.605′N, 119°43.510′W From either South Carson Street or I-580, follow Fairview Drive to the roundabout at East 5th Street and proceed eastbound on 5th for 0.2 mile to Carson River Road. The entrance to the marked trailhead is on the southwest side of the intersection immediately after turning right onto Carson River Road. Park your vehicle in the large dirt area near the start of the trail. The trailhead is equipped with a vault toilet and shade structure with picnic table.

TRAIL | From the westernmost gate near the start of an old dirt road, head to the right (northwest) on a single-track trail and a mild to moderate climb up a slope covered with typical sagebrush scrub. Soon the trail arcs around to cross back over the road and heads south and then southwest, paralleling the old roadbed just to your right. Reach a Y junction [2], where the Sagebrush Loop heads east at 0.3 mile from the trailhead. For a quick and easy trip, follow the Sagebrush Loop 0.4 mile back to the parking area.

Continue ahead from the junction onto the Rabbitbrush Loop, soon passing to the left of a circular pile of rocks before reaching the next junction [3] at 0.5 mile. Here the Bitterbrush Loop goes both ahead (southwest) and also to the upper left (southeast), while the Rabbitbrush Loop veers to the lower left (east). For a 1.1-mile option, take the east side of the Rabbitbrush and Sagebrush Loops back to the trailhead.

To continue the counterclockwise circuit for the full loop, proceed ahead from the junction on a steeper climb another 0.1 mile to a junction [4] with a short trail on your right. Follow this path west up toward a low rock outcrop to Scout Viewpoint [5] at the high point of the trip, where a nearby metal park bench (the result of an Eagle Scout project) offers the opportunity to sit and enjoy the westward view across the valley of the

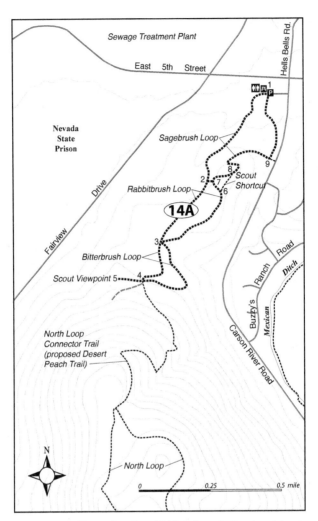

14A. Prison Hill: Sagebrush, Rabbitbrush, and Bitterbrush Loop

Carson Range, including Slide Mountain, Snow Valley Peak, and C Hill. After thoroughly enjoying the vista, retrace your steps to the junction. [4] (At the junction, for a longer trip, follow the narrower track of the North Loop Connector steeply uphill to the south across the hillside ahead and onward to a connection with the North Loop.)

To resume the loop trip, veer sharply east on the continuation of the Bitterbrush Loop on a gentle descent toward the east side of Prison Hill, where views of the Carson River valley and the Pine Nut Mountains beyond are featured more prominently. Reach the four-way junction, [3] where the

Desert Peach blossoms

Bitterbrush and Rabbitbrush Loops converge. Turn right (east) and proceed along the east flank of the hill. The next junction [6] is with the Scout Shortcut near the 1.25-mile mark. Bend to the left (northwest) here and soon encounter the next junction, [7] 1.4 miles from the trailhead, where a very short lateral angling behind and to the left connects to the junction [2] at the west side of the Rabbitbrush and Sagebrush Loops.

Bend to the right (northeast) to remain on the counterclockwise loop circuit on a brief climb to where a very short path leads to another viewpoint [8] with a metal park bench (also placed by the Eagle Scout), where additional views to the north and east offer another temptation to sit and enjoy the scenery.

Follow gently descending tread away from the viewpoint and bend over toward an alternate access point [9] from Carson River Road at 1.6 miles. From there, turn north and follow the fence line west of the road before winding tread leads downhill back to close the loop at the parking area. [1]

> **DESERT PEACH** (*Prunus adnersonii*) A deciduous shrub in the rose family, desert peach is a common plant in the sagebrush scrub community of the foothills. Growing to heights of over six feet, the plant is easily recognized in spring, when branches are full of small pink flowers. Mainly rodents eat the small apricot-colored fruits.

1: Start at trailhead; **2:** Straight at junction; **3:** Straight at junction; **4:** Reach junction to Scout Viewpoint; **5:** Scout Viewpoint; **4:** Return to junction, turn left; **3:** Turn right at junction; **6:** Left at Scout Shortcut junction; **7:** Turn right at junction; **8:** Straight at junction; **9:** Left at Carson River Road junction; **1:** Return to trailhead.

OPTIONS | As Prison Hill boasts a fine network of trails, extending your trip is straightforward. The most obvious extension would be to continue south on the North Loop Trail, which adds about 3 miles to your trip back to the North Loop Connector trailhead.

14B ▪ North Loop

LEVEL	Hike, intermediate
LENGTH	4.0 miles, lollipop loop
TIME	1/2 day
ELEVATION	+800'/–800'
USERS	Hikers, trail runners, mountain bikers, equestrians
DOGS	OK
DIFFICULTY	Moderate
SEASON	All year
BEST TIMES	Spring, fall
FACILITIES	None
MAP	Carson City: *Prison Hill Recreation Area and Silver Saddle Ranch* (https://www.carson.org/home/showdocument?id =38830)
MANAGEMENT	Carson City Parks, Recreation, and Open Space at 775-887-2262, www.carson.org/government/departments-g-z/parks -recreation-open-space
HIGHLIGHTS	Views
LOWLIGHTS	Exposed to sun—hot in summer

TIP | Given Prison Hill's lack of trees, users who visit in the summer or at other times of the year when high temperatures are forecast should take the proper precautions, using sunblock on exposed skin and carrying plenty of fluids.

KID TIP | The four-mile North Loop may not be the best choice for small children on Prison Hill. Perhaps consider the West Loop as an alternative.

TRAILHEAD | 39°08.142′N, 119°44.274′E From either South Carson Street or I-580, follow Fairview Drive east to South Edmonds Drive and turn right. Continue on Edmonds for 1.3 miles to Koontz Lane. Turn left and follow the dirt road uphill toward a water tank, veering to the left of the tank on the way to the trailhead parking area.

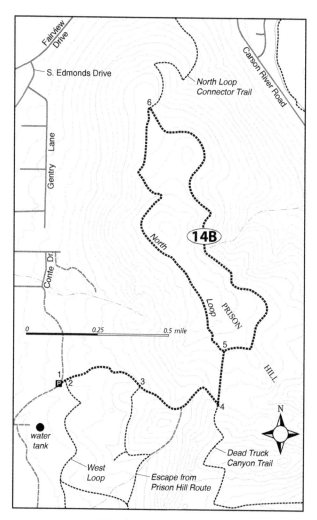

14B. Prison Hill: North Loop

TRAIL | Just after passing through a gap in a fence, you reach a junction [2] with the West Loop on the right. Continue ahead on a gentle climb that soon becomes stiffer on the way into a small canyon. Reach the lower junction [3] of the Escape from Prison Hill Route on the right and continue uphill on a moderately steep climb on rocky tread to the head of the canyon, where the grade eases on the way to the next junction with the Dead Truck Canyon Trail on the right. [4]

Turn left (north) and follow the shared route of the North Loop and Escape from Prison Hill Route, enjoying fine views to the west of Carson

City and the Carson Range beyond. A 0.2-mile, moderate ascent leads to a junction [5] at the start of the loop section, 1.1 miles from the trailhead.

Turn left and follow a well-defined, single-track trail on a winding climb up to the top of a hillside, where you make an easy traverse to the northwest. Good views complement the easy hiking on this stretch of trail for about 0.4 mile, followed by a stiff descent on the way to a three-way junction [6] with the North Loop Connector Trail at 2.2 miles.

Remaining on the North Loop, you angle back to the southeast from the junction and make a moderate climb with views of the ranchland to the east bordering the Carson River and the Pine Nut Mountains beyond. Proceed through widely scattered junipers to a lengthy, mildly undulating traverse across open slopes with more excellent views. Spring visitors may see a sprinkling of wildflowers along this part of the journey. Toward the end of the long traverse, the trail makes a short, steep climb over the top of Prison Hill just to the north of point 5390, where the peaks of the Carson Range spring back into view. A short but stiff descent leads back to the loop junction. [5] From there, retrace your steps to the trailhead. [1]

MILESTONES

1: Start at trailhead; **2:** Straight at junction; **3:** Straight at junction; **4:** Left at junction; **5:** Left at North Loop junction; **6:** Right at North Loop Connector junction; **5:** Right at North Loop junction; **1:** Return to trailhead.

OPTIONS | Connections to other trails of the Prison Hill network would allow you to easily extend your journey even farther.

14C ▪ West Loop

LEVEL	Hike, intermediate
LENGTH	2.5 miles, lollipop loop
TIME	1 to 2 hours
ELEVATION	+200'/−200'
USERS	Hikers, trail runners, mountain bikers, equestrians
DOGS	OK
DIFFICULTY	Easy to moderate
SEASON	All year
BEST TIMES	Spring, fall
FACILITIES	None
MAP	Carson City: *Prison Hill Recreation Area and Silver Saddle Ranch* (https://www.carson.org/home/showdocument?id=38830)
MANAGEMENT	Carson City Parks, Recreation, and Open Space at 775-887-2262, www.carson.org/government/departments-g-z/parks-recreation-open-space

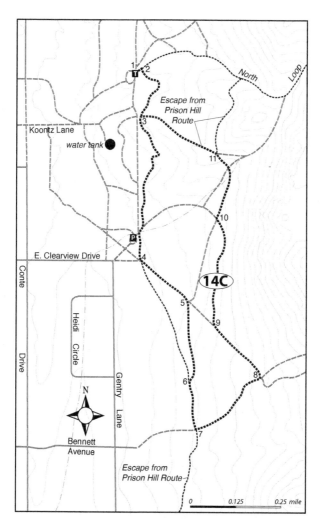

14C. Prison Hill: West Loop

HIGHLIGHTS Views

LOWLIGHTS Exposed to sun—hot in summer

TIP I Given Prison Hill's lack of trees, users who visit in the summer or at other times of the year when high temperatures are forecast should take the proper precautions, using sunblock on exposed skin and carrying plenty of fluids.

KID TIP I The relatively short West Loop may present a fine opportunity to introduce youngsters to the activity of hiking, provided it's not a forced march during the scorching heat of an afternoon summer day. Since there isn't any shade, keep plenty of liquids and sunscreen on hand even in cooler seasons. In spring, the seasonal drainages may have enough water to provide areas of interesting exploration for kids.

TRAILHEAD | 39°08.142′N, 119°44.274′E From either South Carson Street or I-580, follow Fairview Drive east to South Edmonds Drive and turn right. Continue on Edmonds for 1.3 miles to Koontz Lane. Turn left and follow the dirt road uphill toward a water tank, veering to the left of the tank on the way to the trailhead parking area.

TRAIL | Just after passing through a gap in a fence, you reach a junction [2] with the North Loop straight ahead. Turn right, immediately cross a usually dry wash, and head south on a single-track trail on the way to a faint junction [3] with the Escape from Prison Hill Route on the left. (This will also be your return route.) Continue ahead on the more heavily used trail, which is now the shared path of the West Loop and Escape from Prison Hill Route. Near the 0.5-mile point, you intersect a stretch of dirt road and follow it toward an alternate trailhead at the end of Duarte Drive. Just before reaching a fence, you follow a single-track trail bending away to the south for a short distance to soon reach a Y junction marked by a post. [4] Here the West Loop and Escape from Prison Hill Route temporarily diverge.

To remain on the West Loop, take the left-hand trail and head southeast on a gentle ascent that soon becomes steeper on the way to a four-way junction. [5] Veer to the right here and head due south to a three-way junction, [6] where the West Loop rejoins the Escape from Prison Hill Route. Proceed ahead for 0.1 mile to another junction, [7] where the West Loop veers sharply away to the left and the Escape from Prison Hill Route continues ahead to the south. From this slightly elevated perch, you have fine views to the south of the Carson Valley and some of the Carson Range peaks.

Veering left, a steady uphill climb leads to yet another junction [8] with a maze of roads—fortunately some signs help to keep you on track, as you turn to the northwest and head slightly downhill while enjoying sweeping views across Eagle Valley to Slide Mountain and the hills of the Carson Range. Reach a signed Y junction [9] and bend to the right with continuous views as your companion. Traverse the upper slopes of Prison Hill on the way to the crossing of a well-used trail heading downslope. Proceed ahead from this intersection and soon merge with an old road from above, which you follow for a bit to an unmarked junction. [10] (Here the road bends and proceeds downhill to an alternate trailhead at Duarte Drive.) Follow the single-track trail on the right and head north-northeast toward the bottom of a gully with a road running through it. A short climb out of this gully brings you to a junction [11] where a left-hand turn leads northeast along the shared path of the West Loop and Escape from Prison Hill Route to the close of the loop at the junction. [3] From there, turn right and simply retrace your steps the short distance to the trailhead. [1]

MILESTONES

1: Start at trailhead; 2: Right at North Loop junction; 3: Straight at junction; 4: Left at Y junction; 5: Right at four-way junction; 6: Straight at three-way junction; 7: Sharp left at Escape from Prison Hill junction; 8: Left at junction; 9: Right at Y junction; 10: Right at junction; 11: Left at junction; 3: Right at loop junction; 1: Return to trailhead.

OPTIONS | With so many interconnecting trails and roads along the West Loop, your greatest task may be staying on route. However, these numerous tracks offer plenty of options for further wanderings. Fortunately, the open terrain allows you to constantly maintain your bearings; getting lost would be extremely difficult.

14D ▪ Point 5585

LEVEL	Hike, intermediate
LENGTH	2.5 miles, out and back
TIME	1 to 2 hours
ELEVATION	+650'/−0'
USERS	Hikers, trail runners, mountain bikers, equestrians
DOGS	OK
DIFFICULTY	Easy to moderate
SEASON	All year
BEST TIMES	Spring, fall
FACILITIES	None
MAP	Carson City: *Prison Hill Recreation Area and Silver Saddle Ranch* (https://www.carson.org/home/showdocument?id=38830)
MANAGEMENT	Carson City Parks, Recreation, and Open Space at 775-887-2262, www.carson.org/government/departments-g-z/parks-recreation-open-space
HIGHLIGHTS	Views
LOWLIGHTS	Exposed to sun—hot in summer

TIP | Given Prison Hill's lack of trees, users who visit in the summer or at other times of the year when high temperatures are forecast should take the proper precautions, using sunblock on exposed skin and carrying plenty of fluids.

KID TIP | The stiff climb to the top of Prison Hill may not be the best choice for small children. Perhaps consider the West Loop as an alternative.

Wildflowers and rock outcrops from the trail

TRAILHEAD | 39°08.142′N, 119°44.274′W From either South Carson Street or I-580, follow Fairview Drive east to South Edmonds Drive and turn right. Continue on Edmonds for 1.3 miles to Koontz Lane. Turn left and follow the dirt road uphill toward a water tank, veering to the left of the tank on the way to the trailhead parking area.

TRAIL | Just after passing through a gap in a fence, you reach a junction **[2]** with the West Loop on the right. Continue ahead on a gentle climb that soon

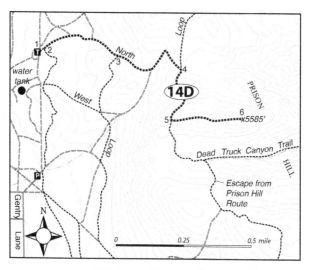

14D. Prison Hill: Point 5585

Hikers gaze upward to Point 5585

becomes stiffer on the way into a small canyon. Reach the lower junction [3] of the Escape from Prison Hill Route on the right and continue uphill on a moderately steep climb on rocky tread to the head of the canyon, where the grade eases on the way to the next junction with the Dead Truck Canyon Trail on the right. [4]

Turn right and follow a slightly winding, stiff ascent up the hillside on the way to a three-way junction [5] where the road, which remains the joint route of the Dead Truck Canyon Trail and Escape from Prison Hill Route, continues ahead.

Take the left-hand trail away from the junction and follow mildly rising tread along the ridge crest to the high point of Prison Hill. [6] Here, at 5,585 feet, you have marvelous views in all directions, with the Carson Range lining Eagle and Carson Valleys to the west and the Pine Nut Mountains to the east beyond the Carson River valley. When the time comes, retrace your steps to the trailhead. [1]

PRISON HILL In the early 1860s, a hotel and some swimming pools were located near hot springs at the base of what would become known as Prison Hill. Abraham Curry was the proprietor, who served the loggers and miners who worked in the area, as well as travelers passing through. In 1862, the hotel was leased to serve as the Territorial Prison, and Mr. Curry was its first warden. Later, the state purchased the land and built a more modern facility. Inmates from the prison quarried sandstone from the north end of Prison Hill, which was then used to build many of Carson City's buildings, including the capitol and US mint, as well as the prison itself. In addition, rock from the quarry was used in Reno, Virginia City, and the Brunswick Mill.

MILESTONES
1: Start at trailhead; 2: Straight at West Loop junction; 3: Straight at junction; 4: Right at junction; 5: Left at junction; 6: Top of Prison Hill; 1: Return to junction.

GO GREEN | Muscle Powered is the preeminent organization for building and maintaining trails in Carson City. Established in 1999, the group has been an unparalleled advocate for biking and hiking trails in the area. Along with trail building and maintenance, education, and advocacy, the nonprofit group also hosts community events. They routinely sponsor trash mobs, cleanup projects that make a valuable contribution to the beautification of the greater Carson City area. You can become a member and support the work at www.musclepowered.org.

OPTIONS | With two vehicles, you could create a point-to-point trip by ending at Silver Saddle Ranch.

Carson River Park

Located on the banks of the Carson River immediately east of Prison Hill, forty-acre Carson River Park is a sleepy haven offering a gentle circuit through old ranchlands. The park is also well suited as a jumping-off point for an easy stroll along a stretch of the Mexican Ditch to its origin at the dam of the same name.

15A ▪ Park Loop

LEVEL	Walk, novice
LENGTH	1.9 miles, loop
TIME	1 hour
ELEVATION	Negligible
USERS	Hikers, trail runners, mountain bikers, equestrians
DOGS	OK
DIFFICULTY	Easy
SEASON	All year
BEST TIMES	Spring, fall
FACILITIES	Boat ramp (nonmotorized), handicap-accessible fishing pier, interpretive signs, picnic tables (covered), portable toilet, trash cans
MAP	Carson City: *Prison Hill Recreation Area and Silver Saddle Ranch* (https://www.carson.org/home/showdocument?id=38830)
MANAGEMENT	Carson City Parks, Recreation, and Open Space at 775-887-2262, www.carson.org/government/departments-g-z/parks-recreation-open-space
HIGHLIGHTS	Autumn color, ditch, river, wildlife
LOWLIGHTS	Exposed to sun—hot in summer

TIP ׀ The park is open during daylight hours.

KID TIP ׀ Carson River Park is a great place for kids to learn about riparian ecology in a fun setting along the banks of the Carson River. However, with the river so close by, small children must be under constant supervision,

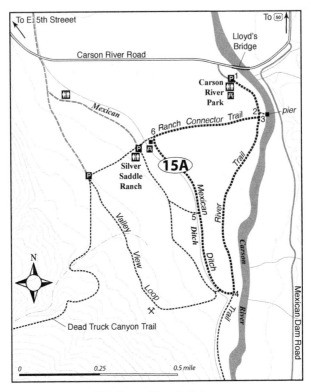

15A. Carson River Park Loop

especially when the river is running high. A picnic lunch at the park would offer a fine conclusion to your hike.

TRAILHEAD | 39°08.491′N, 119°42.337′W Follow East 5th Street 0.2 mile from the roundabout at Fairview Drive to Carson River Road and turn right. Continue 2 miles to the entrance into Carson River Park, which is immediately before a bridge over the Carson River. Park your vehicle in the paved parking lot.

TRAIL | Begin your walk by passing around a closed steel gate and following the River Trail on the decomposed granite surface of an old road bordering a cottonwood-lined stretch of the Carson River on the left and a verdant pocket of fenced pastureland on the right. Across the pasture are the historic buildings of Silver Saddle Ranch, towered over by the east slope of Prison Hill. Head along the nearly level road a short way to a Y junction. [2] The left-hand path leads over to the river, where you'll find a couple of picnic tables and the handicap-accessible fishing pier. Beyond the Y junction, you

Carson River Park is a fine place to expose children to the outdoors

pass through a gate near an irrigation ditch and reach a junction **[3]** with an old road on the right that heads across the pasture. (This will be the return route.) Continue upstream along the river to a Y junction near the 0.5-mile mark, where a road comes in from behind on the right. Proceed to a junction **[4]** near an open steel gate, 0.7 mile from the trailhead, where the old road meets the Mexican Ditch Trail just before a spillway that funnels excess water from the ditch back into the river.

Turn right and follow the Mexican Ditch Trail away from the edge of the river and the intermittent shade provided by the cottonwoods. Shortly the trail bends northwest and meets the east bank of the Mexican Ditch, where a wood plank leads across the ditch and connects to the system of old roads coursing through Silver Saddle Ranch. You continue ahead on the Mexican Ditch Trail, traveling across a section of pastureland no longer being irrigated. A barbed-wire fence runs along the east bank of the ditch, which is lined with sagebrush scrub and an occasional Russian olive tree. Around the three-mile mark, you reach a junction, **[5]** where a gate provides access to a stout, wood-rail bridge leading across the ditch and connecting with an old road headed toward the buildings of Silver Saddle Ranch.

Continue ahead at the junction to a fence line, where the Mexican Ditch Trail intersects a twin-tracked road coming in on the right near an active irrigation ditch. Beyond this point, follow the ditch alongside irrigated pastureland on a sweeping bend toward the buildings at the main part of the ranch. Soon you reach the old, cottonwood-shaded ranch house and associated outbuildings, where interpretive signs offer glimpses into the history of the area. Intersect the main access road at the far end of the ranch house property [6] and turn right onto a road heading east across the pasture.

Follow the road in between a pair of fences on a straight line across the pasturelands to where you intersect the River Trail at the close of the loop. [2] From there, simply retrace your steps to the trailhead. [1]

MILESTONES

1: Start at trailhead; **2:** Straight at fishing pier junction; **3:** Straight at junction; **4:** Right at Mexican Ditch junction; **5:** Straight at bridge junction; **6:** Right at ranch house road; **3:** Left at River Trail junction; **1:** Return to trailhead.

OPTIONS Connections to Silver Saddle Ranch offer plenty of options for trip extensions.

15B ▪ River and Mexican Ditch Trails to Mexican Dam

LEVEL	Walk, novice
LENGTH	3 miles, out and back
TIME	1 to 1-1/2 hours
ELEVATION	Negligible
USERS	Hikers, trail runners, mountain bikers, equestrians
DOGS	OK
DIFFICULTY	Easy
SEASON	All year
BEST TIMES	Spring, fall
FACILITIES	Boat ramp (nonmotorized), handicap-accessible fishing pier, interpretive signs, picnic tables (covered), portable toilet, trash cans
MAP	Carson City: *Prison Hill Recreation Area and Silver Saddle Ranch* (https://www.carson.org/home/showdocument?id=38830)
MANAGEMENT	Carson City Parks, Recreation, and Open Space at 775-887-2262, www.carson.org/government/departments-g-z/parks-recreation-open-space
HIGHLIGHTS	Autumn color, ditch, river, wildlife
LOWLIGHTS	Exposed to sun—hot in summer

TIP The park is open during daylight hours.

KID TIP Carson River Park is a great place for kids to learn about riparian ecology in a fun setting along the banks of the Carson River. However, with

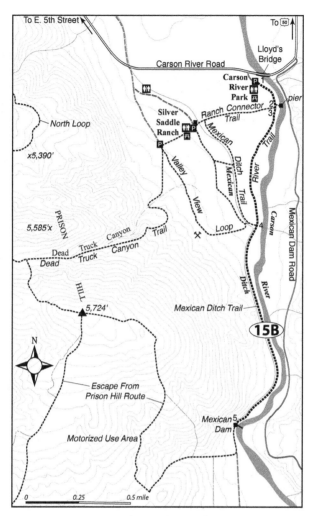

15B. Carson River Park to Mexican Dam

the river and ditch so close by, small children must be under constant supervision, especially when the river is running high. A picnic lunch at the park would offer a fine conclusion to your hike.

TRAILHEAD | 39°08.491′N, 119°42.337′W Follow East 5th Street 0.2 mile from the roundabout at Fairview Drive to Carson River Road and turn right. Continue 2 miles to the entrance to Carson River Park, which is immediately before a bridge over the Carson River. Park your vehicle in the paved parking lot.

Autumn color along a stretch of the Carson River

TRAIL ⏐ Begin your walk by passing around a closed steel gate and following the River Trail on the decomposed granite surface of an old road bordering a cottonwood-lined stretch of the Carson River on the left and a verdant pocket of fenced pastureland on the right. Across the pasture are the historic buildings of Silver Saddle Ranch, towered over by the east slope of Prison Hill. Head along the nearly level road a short way to a Y junction. [2] The left-hand path leads over to the river, where you'll find a couple of picnic tables and the handicap-accessible fishing pier. Beyond the Y junction, you pass through a gate near an irrigation ditch and reach a junction [3] with an old road on the right that heads across the pasture. (This will be the return route.) Continue upstream along the river to a Y junction near the 0.5-mile mark, where a road comes in from behind on the right. Proceed to a junction [4] near an open steel gate, 0.7 mile from the trailhead, where the old road meets the Mexican Ditch Trail just before a spillway that funnels excess water from the ditch back into the river.

Continue ahead from the junction and follow the course of the ditch that roughly parallels the river. The nearly level grade of the old roadway makes for easy walking, which allows the miles to click by fairly rapidly. At 1.5 miles from the trailhead, you reach the site of the dam. One of the proposed improvements for this area includes a safer and easier way across the dam. From there, retrace your steps to the trailhead. [1]

Mexican Dam

MEXICAN DAM AND DITCH A group of Mexican nationals undertook an ambitious project to divert water from the Carson River to the Mexican Mill located farther downstream near the head of Brunswick Canyon (at the present-day site of the Empire Ranch Golf Course). The water-and-steam-powered mill processed ore from the Comstock Lode, processing up to seventy-five tons a day until closing in 1885. The Mexicans constructed a stone dam across the river in the early 1860s, which sent water to the mill via a nearly four-mile ditch that was fifteen feet wide at the top and eight feet wide at the bottom, with a grade of one foot per mile. As with most water projects in the region, competing interests waged contentious court battles over water rights over the years; despite the miners achieving a legal victory, ranchers eventually won the war when the local mining economy collapsed in the early 1900s. The water is currently still used for irrigation purposes.

MILESTONES
1: Start at trailhead; **2:** Straight at fishing pier junction; **3:** Straight at junction; **4:** Straight at Mexican Ditch junction; **5:** Mexican Dam; **1:** Return to trailhead.

GO GREEN | A branch of the Carson City Historical Society, the Foundation for the Betterment of Carson City Parks and Recreation (The Park Foundation) is an independent, nonprofit organization working with government, community groups, and like-minded organizations to support and enhance the area's parks. For more information, consult their website at www.cchistorical .org/parkfoundation2.htm.

OPTIONS | Connections to Silver Saddle Ranch offer plenty of options for trip extensions.

16 Silver Saddle Ranch

Once slated for development, the 703-acre Silver Saddle Ranch was saved via a land exchange and was opened to the public in 2000. Acquired by the BLM, the property is in the process of being conveyed to Carson City and is protected from future development by a conservation easement. Recreationists have their choice from a handful of trails that follow old ranch roads and sections of single-track trail across the property. The Mexican Ditch Trail is a basically flat route that parallels the ditch from the ranch house for almost 1.5 miles to the Mexican Dam on the Carson River. The Valley View Loop makes a 1.3-mile circuit across nonirrigated land above the ditch with fine views of the ranch, river, and mountains of the Pine Nut Range. The Dead Truck Canyon Trail, so named for the presence of a rusting old pickup truck, offers a stiff climb away from the ranch to sweeping views of the surrounding terrain at the top of Prison Hill.

16A ▪ Mexican Ditch Trail to Mexican Dam

LEVEL	Walk, novice
LENGTH	2.8 miles, out and back
TIME	1 to 1-1/2 hours
ELEVATION	Negligible
USERS	Hikers, trail runners, mountain bikers, equestrians
DOGS	OK
DIFFICULTY	Easy
SEASON	All year
BEST TIMES	Spring, fall
FACILITIES	Interpretive signs, picnic tables, trash cans, vault toilet
MAP	Carson City: *Prison Hill Recreation Area and Silver Saddle Ranch* (https://www.carson.org/home/showdocument?id =38830)
MANAGEMENT	Carson City Parks, Recreation, and Open Space at 775-887-2262, www.carson.org/government/departments-g-z/parks -recreation-open-space

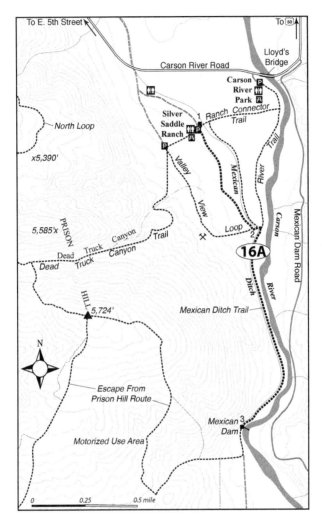

16A. Silver Saddle Ranch to Mexican Dam

HIGHLIGHTS Autumn color, ditch, history, river, wildlife

LOWLIGHTS Exposed to sun—hot in summer

TIP The park is open during daylight hours.

KID TIP Silver Saddle Ranch is a great place for kids to learn about riparian ecology in a fun setting along the banks of the Carson River. However, with the river and ditch so close by, small children must be under constant supervision, especially when the river is running high. A picnic lunch at the ranch would offer a fine conclusion to your hike.

A family enjoys a bike ride at Silver Saddle Ranch

TRAILHEAD | 39°08.327′N, 119°42.700′W Follow East 5th Street 0.2 mile from the roundabout at Fairview Drive to Carson River Road and turn right. Continue 1.4 miles to the entrance into Silver Saddle Ranch and proceed 0.4 mile on the access road to a sharp left-hand turn. Continue another 0.2 mile to the dirt parking area behind some ranch buildings.

TRAIL | Begin your hike by walking to the southeast corner of the ranch house property, [2] where a twin-tracked road on your right heads generally south along the fringe of an irrigated pasture. Follow the road as it soon meets the fenced Mexican Ditch on your right and bends southeast alongside the waterway. After a quarter mile, you reach a junction [3] near a ditch running east-west at the south end of the irrigated pasture, where a road angles away to the left toward the Carson River. Go straight at the junction to follow the Mexican Ditch road bending south, and continue a short way farther to a three-way junction [4] where a gate on the right provides access to a stout, wood-rail bridge across the ditch leading to an old road headed back toward the buildings at Silver Saddle Ranch. Continue ahead as the ditch eventually bends southeast and comes to another junction, [5] this one with a route that crosses a plank bridge over the ditch and connects to a road back to the ranch. From the junction, the Mexican Ditch Trail makes a sharp bend to the left and travels a short distance toward the river to meet the River Trail [6] from Carson River Park.

Continue upstream (southwest) from the junction and soon rejoin the Mexican Ditch near a spillway that sends excess water from the ditch back into the river. Follow the course of the ditch roughly paralleling the river upstream. The nearly level grade of the old roadway makes for easy walking, which allows the miles to click by fairly rapidly. At 1.4 miles from the trailhead, you reach the site of the dam. One of the proposed improvements for this area includes a safer and easier way across the dam. [7] From there, retrace your steps to the trailhead.

MILESTONES

1: Start at trailhead; 2: Right at ranch house; 3: Straight at junction; 4: Straight at three-way junction; 5: Left at junction; 6: Right at River Trail junction; 7: Mexican Dam; 1: Return to trailhead.

OPTIONS | To add some variety to the trip, you could alter your return from the dam by taking the River Trail north to the Ranch Connector Trail and then traveling west back to Silver Saddle Ranch.

16B ▪ Valley View Loop

LEVEL	Walk, novice
LENGTH	1.3 miles, loop
TIME	1 hour
ELEVATION	+100'/−100'
USERS	Hikers, trail runners, equestrians
DOGS	OK
DIFFICULTY	Easy
SEASON	All year
BEST TIMES	Spring, fall
FACILITIES	Interpretive signs, picnic tables, trash cans, vault toilet
MAP	Carson City: *Prison Hill Recreation Area and Silver Saddle Ranch* (https://www.carson.org/home/showdocument?id=38830)
MANAGEMENT	Carson City Parks, Recreation, and Open Space at 775-887-2262, www.carson.org/government/departments-g-z/parks-recreation-open-space
HIGHLIGHTS	Autumn color, ditch, history, river, wildlife
LOWLIGHTS	Exposed to sun—hot in summer

TIP | The park is open during daylight hours.

KID TIP | This loop is short and not physically demanding, which makes the trip suitable for kids. The Silver Saddle Ranch house and surrounding structures should offer an opportunity to engage them about the human history of the area. The old mine site might provide a place to poke around under

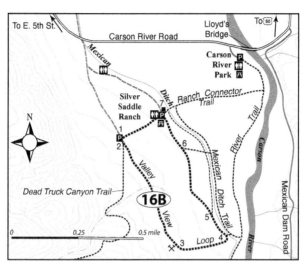

16B. Silver Saddle Ranch to Valley View

adult supervision as a way to introduce the mining history of the Comstock Lode. For further adventures, consider visiting the Children's Museum of Northern Nevada (813 North Carson St.) after your hike. For more information, consult the website at www.cmnn.org.

TRAILHEAD | 39°08.134′N, 119°42.591′W Follow East 5th Street 0.2 mile from the roundabout at Fairview Drive to Carson River Road and turn right. Continue 1.4 miles to the entrance into Silver Saddle Ranch and proceed 0.4 mile on the access road to the small trailhead parking area near a sharp left-hand turn.

TRAIL | From the parking area, head southbound for a short distance to a junction [2] where the Valley Loop Trail veers left (southeast). Follow the wide track of an old ranch road on a mildly rising ascent through sagebrush scrub, passing by any side trails that seem to come and go en route to the site of an old mine [3] tucked into a hillside on the right. Lacking signs to guide you, the indistinct route from the mine site heading downhill to the east may be hard to locate at first. However, a stretch of single-track trail does indeed drop down the hillside away from the mine and crosses a sagebrush slope to a four-way junction [4] with a road paralleling the west side of the Mexican Ditch. Here, the path ahead leads to a bridge over the ditch and a junction with the River Trail from Carson River Park.

Turning left, you follow the ditch briefly northwest to the next junction, [5] where a fainter track continues along the ditch, but you veer left, remaining on the more distinct road. Soon the road bends north and comes to a junction [6] with a road on the right heading southeast to a bridge over the ditch and a connection to the Mexican Ditch Trail. Continuing on the road, you walk to a gate at a corral, stroll across the corral to another gate on the far side, and then proceed on a road between the ranch's outbuildings to where the access road appears on the left. [7]

Turn right and climb up the access road about 0.2 mile to the parking lot and the close of the loop. [1]

MILESTONES

1: Start at trailhead; 2: Veer left at Dead Truck Canyon junction; 3: Left at mine site; 4: Left at junction; 5: Straight at junction; 6: Straight a junction; 7: Left at access road junction; 1: Return to trailhead.

16C ▪ Dead Truck Canyon to Silver Saddle Overlook

LEVEL	Hike, intermediate
LENGTH	3.4 miles, loop
TIME	2 hours
ELEVATION	+1,000′/–0′
USERS	Hikers, trail runners, mountain bikers, equestrians
DOGS	OK
DIFFICULTY	Strenuous
SEASON	All year
BEST TIMES	Spring, fall
FACILITIES	Interpretive signs, picnic tables, trash cans, vault toilet
MAP	Carson City: *Prison Hill Recreation Area and Silver Saddle Ranch* (https://www.carson.org/home/showdocument?id =38830)
MANAGEMENT	Carson City Parks, Recreation, and Open Space at 775-887-2262, www.carson.org/government/departments-g-z/parks -recreation-open-space
HIGHLIGHTS	Summit, views
LOWLIGHTS	Exposed to sun—hot in summer

TIP | The park is open during daylight hours.

KID TIP | The steep grade and sometimes poor tread of this hike probably make this trip unsuitable for small children. Consider the other trips at Silver Saddle Ranch as better alternatives.

TRAILHEAD | 39°08.134′N, 119°42.591′W Follow East 5th Street 0.2 mile from the roundabout at Fairview Drive to Carson River Road and turn right. Continue 1.4 miles to the entrance into Silver Saddle Ranch and proceed 0.4 mile on the access road to the small trailhead parking area near a sharp left-hand turn.

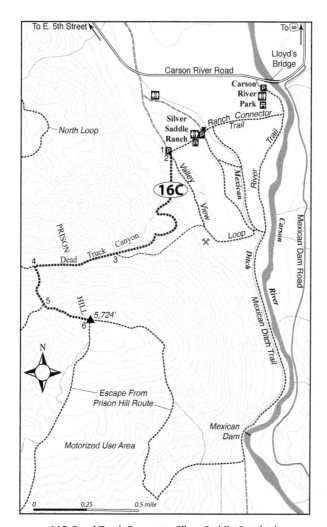

16C. Dead Truck Canyon to Silver Saddle Overlook

TRAIL | From the parking area, head south for a short distance to a junction where the Valley Loop Trail veers left (southeast), but you take the right-hand path initially heading south through typical sagebrush scrub vegetation. After about 0.3 mile, the trail bends southwest to enter the lower end of Dead Truck Canyon and soon crosses over the usually dry wash. The route of the trail climbs out of the wash and arcs up the hillside to the crest of a rocky knoll near the 0.5-mile point with fine views of Silver Saddle Ranch, a stretch of the Carson River below, and the Pine Nut Mountains beyond. From there, the trail climbs back into the canyon and comes to a marked

Coyote

junction [2] at 0.75 mile, where an old road angles back to the left. Proceed ahead from the junction, basically climbing directly up the wash amid low rock outcrops and very widely scattered pinyon pines. Reach a T junction [3] at 1.2 miles, where the Dead Truck Canyon Trail continues ahead.

Leaving the Dead Truck Canyon Trail, you turn left at the junction and climb steeply to the south up to a saddle and a junction [4] with a road heading southwest. Veer to the left at the junction and resume the stiff climb south-southeast to the high point of Prison Hill [5] at 5,724 feet. The view from the summit is sweeping, with the Carson Range delineating the eastern escarpment of the mighty Sierra Nevada to the west, towering over Carson City and Eagle Valley. To the east above the verdant plain along the Carson River stand the hills of the Pine Nut Mountains. After plenty of time to take in the marvelous view, retrace your steps to the trailhead. [1]

COYOTE (*Canis latrans*) Perhaps no wild animal has adapted to the urbanization of the West better than this member of the canine family. Originally confined to the central United States and northern Mexico, coyotes have expanded their range all across the continent, due primarily to the eradication of their chief competitor, the wolf. Weighing between twenty and forty pounds, they are opportunistic hunters in the wild, surviving mainly on rabbits, rodents, and carrion. Coyotes close to urban areas will raid garbage cans and prey on cats and small dogs when available. In contrast to legend, coyotes don't usually hunt in packs, preferring to hunt alone or with a mate. In urban settings, you're most likely to see an individual early in the morning or around sunset, whereas in the wild, they typically hunt during the day.

MILESTONES

1: Start at trailhead; **2:** Straight at junction; **3:** Left at T junction; **4:** Left at junction in saddle; **5:** Top of Prison Hill; **1:** Return to trailhead.

GO GREEN I Incorporated in 2001, Friends of Silver Saddle Ranch is a nonprofit organization dedicated to the preservation of the ranch's cultural, historical, and natural resources. For more information, visit the group's website at www.freindsofssr.org.

OPTIONS I Myriad roads and trails crisscrossing Prison Hill offer plenty of opportunities for further wanderings. The longest designated trail in the area is the Escape from Prison Hill Route. Starting at the Silver Saddle Ranch, the 12.7-mile route follows the Dead Truck Canyon Trail to the North Loop and after completing the loop drops down the west side of Prison Hill to join the north and west sections of the West Loop. From there, the route goes south to the Snyder Avenue trailhead and heads southeast and then north-northeast to Prison Hill's summit. A wandering descent from the summit leads eventually to the Mexican Ditch Trail near the dam and then to the upper section of the Valley Loop Trail before a short loop section ends back at the ranch. The trail is best suited for mountain bikers and trail runners. A half marathon race is held annually in the spring (tahoemtnmilers.org).

Additional Trips

CARSON RIVER TRAILS I Carson City has plans in the works to build a new, approximately two-mile-long trail from the recently improved East 5th Street trailhead along the west side of Carson River Road to a connection with the existing trail network at Silver Saddle Ranch. From there, connecting trails provide further options for longer hikes, including a mile-long section of new trail from Carson River Park north to existing trails in Riverview Park. Construction was slated to begin in 2020.

CHAPTER TWO

THE FOOTHILLS

Where the west edge of Eagle Valley butts into the massive wall of the mighty Carson Range and the north edge melds into the tan-colored hills of the south end of the Virginia Range, the foothills region begins. A transition zone between the sagebrush scrub common to the flatlands and the forests of the upper mountains, the foothills contain a diverse mixture of flora. A transition of human settlement is also present here, as the high-density communities of the city give way to the less populated slopes above. The twelve trips in this chapter range from gently graded treks on old railroad grades to stiff climbs up picturesque canyons and to view-packed summits. In 2018, Carson City acquired 206 acres of property on the west side of town that includes three previously unofficial trails—the Baldy Green, Evidence, and Four Day Trails—making them now legal to hike or ride.

The BLM land above Centennial Park can be both a hiker's dream and nightmare. The land itself certainly has much to offer, with rolling topography and open slopes of sagebrush scrub offering plenty of places to roam with good scenery and fine views. Add in the opportunity to see some of the wild horses that frequent the area, and you have all the makings for an excellent outing minutes from downtown. The downside comes into play from the mishmash of old dirt roads and trails crisscrossing the area without any signage to help keep you on track. However, amid all the poor tread and lack of direction are some well-built and nicely graded sections of single-track tread that are quite enjoyable. The nearly mile-long, initial stretch of trail from the park to the BLM boundary was the result of a senior class project of a Carson High School student, Conner McRae, who continued the work to completion after graduation.

LEVEL	Hike, intermediate
LENGTH	5 miles, loop
TIME	2-1/2 to 3 hours
ELEVATION	+700'/–700'
USERS	Hikers, trail runners, mountain bikers, equestrians
DOGS	OK
DIFFICULTY	Moderate
SEASON	All year
BEST TIME	Spring, fall
FACILITIES	Archery range, ball fields, picnic area, playground, restrooms, tennis courts
MAP	None
MANAGEMENT	Carson City Parks, Recreation, and Open Space at 775-887-2262, www.carson.org/government/departments-g-z/parks-recreation-open-space; Bureau of Land Management at 775-861-6400, www.blm.gov/nv/st/en/fo/carson_city_field.html
HIGHLIGHTS	Scenery, wildlife
LOWLIGHTS	Poorly marked trails, exposed to sun—hot in summer

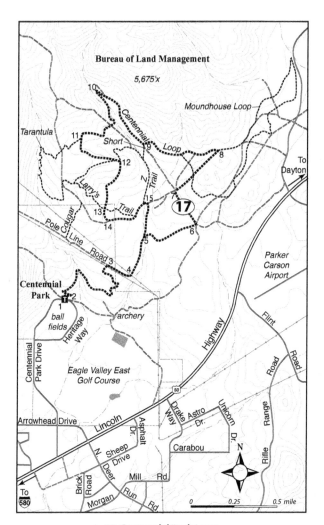

17. Centennial Park Loop

TIP | Due to a lack of signage and poorly delineated trails, staying on course can be a bit challenging.

KID TIP | This loop is not a good choice for small children. The wild horses that frequent the area may fascinate older kids up to the challenge of a five-mile hike under less-than-ideal conditions. Be sure to pack plenty of sunscreen and water.

TRAILHEAD | From downtown or I-580, follow Lincoln Highway (US 50) to a left-hand turn onto Centennial Park Drive. Proceed through the intersection with Arrowhead Drive and follow the road around Eagle Valley Golf Course

View across Eagle Valley of the Carson Range from Centennial Park Loop

to a right turn onto Heritage Way (one-way) and through Centennial Park to the parking lot on the north side of the ball fields. The trail begins near an old faded BLM trail sign.

TRAIL | From the parking area, pass through a gap in a wire fence and follow a gently graded path that immediately crosses a gravel road and comes to a four-by-four post identifying this as the Wildhorse Trail. Proceed generally eastbound past a second post and continue a short distance to a junction [2] marked by a third post. Turn sharply uphill (left) at the junction and then follow a set of switchbacks up a hillside with scattered, low rock outcrops. Above the switchbacks, the trail ascends moderately into a low gully, crosses to the far side, and then follows a rolling traverse generally southeast. Farther on, a winding ascent heads more northerly uphill toward a power line, where you intersect the dirt surface of Pole Line Road [3] near a pair of power poles, 0.9 mile from the trailhead.

Turn right (southeast) and follow the road on a slight descent toward a prominent wash. After 250 yards, where the road curves above the wash, you reach a junction with a single-track trail crossing the road. [4] Leaving the road behind, turn left (uphill) and follow the trail as it parallels the wash on the way to a Y junction with the start of the loop. [5]

Turn to the right, cross over the drainage, and proceed eastbound for 0.3 mile to a four-way junction near the base of a hill. [6] Turn sharply left and go northwest 0.25 mile to a major intersection [7] in a flat, where myriad routes splay out in a variety of directions. Forsake any of the road options here and bend sharply right onto a single-track trail, climbing stiffly up a narrowing draw toward the ridge crest above. After a 0.3-mile ascent, you reach the next junction [8] with a well-traveled dirt road (part of the Moundhouse Loop) at the top of a rise near the southeast base of Peak 5,675.

From the junction, head west on a pleasant traverse across the lower slope of Peak 5,675, a welcome stretch of hiking after the steep climb up the draw. After a brief stint along the road, veer onto a parallel section of single-track trail on the uphill side, enjoying the sweeping views to the south across Eagle Valley to the Carson Range along the way. Optional paths seem to come and go, but generally follow the uphill route to a junction [9] with a well-used road at 2 miles.

Bend to the right and follow the road past a junction with the Short Trail and above a usually dry drainage to your left. Ascend a narrowing canyon, remaining on the road where pieces of single-track trail appear on the left. At 2.6 miles, you forsake the road and follow single-track tread a short distance to the route's high point [10] marked by a rock pile. The hilly topography in the canyon blocks any signs of civilization and emits an away-from-it-all feeling on this part of the loop.

Head downstream, cross over the drainage, climb out of the canyon, and soon cross a dirt road. A pleasantly graded section of single-track trail makes a slightly ascending traverse around the hillside and into the next canyon. Below the head of the canyon, you reach the next junction [11] with the Tarantula Trail heading southwest toward the ridge crest. Continue ahead at the junction, and arc around the hillside on a traverse across the south side of the canyon on the way up to the top of a low ridge, [12] 3.6 miles from the trailhead. Here, the Z Trail bends to the north, and a much fainter stretch of trail heads west-southwest across the ridge.

Take the middle trail and drop stiffly away from the ridge on an arcing descent that bends southwest and then south toward a well-traveled road below, crossing over Larry's Trail [13] along the way. At the bottom, you reach the road [14] and turn left to travel east before bending northeast to reach the wash. [15] Here, you have a few options to consider. While the designated route of the Centennial Loop proceeds from the wash northeast and closes the loop at the major intersection (7), this seems to involve slightly over a 0.5 mile of unnecessary hiking. To avoid the extra distance, either of the single-track paths on either side of the wash heads downstream to the loop junction [5] as described here. (The trail on the far side of the wash is the more distinct of the two.) Once there, simply retrace your steps 0.9 mile to the trailhead. [1]

Red-tailed Hawk

RED-TAILED HAWK (*Buteo jamaicenses*) If you don't see a red-tailed hawk soaring above the canyons, you may hear their characteristic high-pitched, descending screech echoing through the skies. In flight, its rust-colored tail easily identifies this large raptor.

MILESTONES

1: Start at trailhead; **2:** Left at junction; **3:** Right at Pole Line Road; **4:** Left at single-track junction; **5:** Right at loop junction; **6:** Left at five-way junction; **7:** Right at five-way junction; **8:** Left at Moundhouse junction; **9:** Right at road junction; **10:** Loop high point; **11:** Straight at Tarantula junction; **12:** Right at junction; **13:** Straight at Larry's Trail; **14:** Left at road junction; **15:** Right at junction; **5:** Straight at loop junction; **1:** Return to trailhead.

GO GREEN | Muscle Powered is the preeminent organization for building and maintaining trails in Carson City. Established in 1999, the group has been an unparalleled advocate for biking and hiking trails in the area. Along with trail building and maintenance, education, and advocacy, the nonprofit group also hosts community events. They routinely sponsor trash mobs, cleanup projects that make a valuable contribution to the beautification of the greater Carson City area. You can become a member and support the work at www.musclepowered.org.

OPTIONS | The numerous roads and trails crisscrossing the area make extending your trip a straightforward process.

A less developed section of the old V & T Railroad bed than the one described in Trip 11 can be found at the north end of Eagle Valley, north of Coombs Canyon Road. The well-graded trail follows a winding course across the hillside above the Silver Oak Golf Course and continues beyond where construction of the I-580 freeway obliterated the old grade on a section of the newly built Foothill Trail (see Trip 10C), which shortly ends at Hobart Road. *Note: as of 2020, negotiations were ongoing between Carson City and private landowners to make this section of historic trail legal for hikers.*

LEVEL	Walk, intermediate
LENGTH	2.75 miles, shuttle; 5.5 miles, out and back
TIME	1-1/2 hours; 2-1/2 hours
ELEVATION	+300′/−0′
USERS	Hikers, trail runners, mountain bikers, equestrians
DOGS	OK
DIFFICULTY	Easy
SEASON	All year
BEST TIMES	Spring, fall
FACILITIES	None
MAP	Carson City: *Carson City Multi-Use Routes Map*, 4th ed.
MANAGEMENT	Carson City Parks, Recreation, and Open Space at 775-887-2262, www.carson.org/government/departments-g-z/parks-recreation-open-space
HIGHLIGHTS	History
LOWLIGHTS	Exposed to sun—hot in summer

TIP | In summer, get an early start to beat the heat.

KID TIP | After your trip along the old V & T Railroad grade, you could opt for a visit to the Nevada State Railroad Museum, open Thursday to Monday from 9:00 A.M. to 4:00 P.M.; children under seventeen are admitted free. Check out the website for more information at www.nvculture.org/nevadastaterailroadmuseumcarsoncity/.

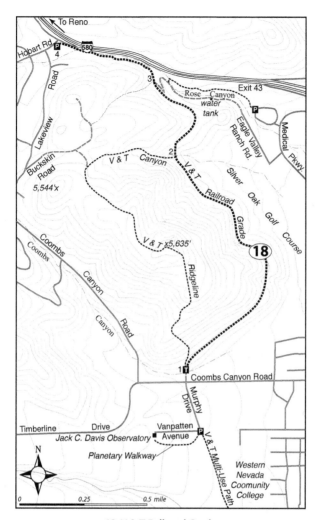

18. V & T Railroad Grade

TRAILHEAD | 39°11.396′N, 119°47.634′W From North Carson Street, turn west onto West College Parkway and travel 0.7 mile to a right turn onto North Ormsby Boulevard. After 0.2 mile, Ormsby turns left and becomes Coombs Canyon Road, which you follow another 0.5 mile to a right turn onto a dirt road at Murphy Drive. Park your vehicle at the end of the road as space allows.

TRAIL | From the Murphy Drive trailhead, the old railroad grade follows a gently rising course on a traverse around the east slopes of Peak 5,635. The journey steadily continues across the hill's minor folds and creases, with fine

Evening view from the V & T Railroad Grade

views across the verdant greens and fairways of the golf course to the distant mountains. After 0.75 mile you reach an unmarked junction, [2] where the V & T Canyon Trail (see Trip 18) veers off to the left to ascend the canyon immediately to the west.

Remaining on the old railroad grade, you continue ahead on an arcing course around point 5,090 to the next junction [3] with a service road down Rose Canyon, 0.2 mile from the previous junction.

Once again, you continue ahead from the junction and climb a bit more steeply to the top of a small bluff above the freeway, where the old grade has disappeared in the wake of the more recent freeway construction. Here, newly built single-track trail slices across the steep hillside above the freeway on a steady upward traverse toward Hobart Road at the end of the trail. [4] With shuttle arrangements, your trip is over; otherwise, retrace your steps to the trailhead.

CALIFORNIA QUAIL (*Callipepia californica*) These plump, highly social birds are most easily identified by their top knot, a teardrop-shaped head plume, which is black on the males and brown on females. Ground dwellers, these birds prefer to run rather than fly, and when they do take to the air, they don't seem to go very far. In the winter, quail tend to band together in groups called coveys. During mating season, they pair up and remain monogamous until the following year, when new

Female California Quail

mates are found. After the chicks are able to fly, in about two weeks, California quail tend to form large family groups again.

MILESTONES

1: Start at trailhead; **2:** Straight at Canyon junction; **3:** Straight at Foothill junction; **4:** Hobart Road.

GO GREEN ∣ Muscle Powered is the preeminent organization for building and maintaining trails in Carson City. Established in 1999, the group has been an unparalleled advocate for biking and hiking trails in the area. Along with trail building and maintenance, education, and advocacy, the nonprofit group also hosts community events. They routinely sponsor trash mobs, cleanup projects that make a valuable contribution to the beautification of the greater Carson City area. You can become a member and support the work at www.musclepowered.org.

OPTIONS ∣ Varying your trip is quite easy by connecting to other trails in the area. The most straightforward extension would be to follow the V & T Canyon and Ridgeline Trails back to the trailhead, reversing the description in Trip 19. Another option involves heading down to Carson Tahoe Hospital (reversing the description in Trip 10C), but this requires either arranging for a shuttle or a long walk between the two trailheads. For even farther wanderings, consider linking up with trails in the Hobart Road system (Trips 48–49).

The V & T Ridgeline Trail starts out with a brutal climb that may intimidate all but the hardiest of hikers. Fortunately, although incredibly steep, the initial ascent is short and the great effort to reach the high point may be quickly forgotten when taking in the wide-ranging view. The route beyond is enjoyably downhill, first on the Canyon Trail and then eventually connecting with the exceedingly pleasantly graded old bed of the V & T Railroad on the way back to the trailhead.

LEVEL	Hike, advanced
LENGTH	3.8 miles, loop
TIME	2 hours
ELEVATION	+650'/−650'
USERS	Hikers, trail runners
DOGS	OK
DIFFICULTY	Strenuous
SEASON	All year
BEST TIMES	Spring, fall
FACILITIES	None
MAP	Carson City: *Carson City Multi-Use Routes Map*, 4th ed.
MANAGEMENT	Carson City Parks, Recreation, and Open Space at 775-887-2262, www.carson.org/government/departments-g-z/parks-recreation-open-space
HIGHLIGHTS	History, summit, views
LOWLIGHTS	Exposed to sun—hot in summer

TIP I Not only is the initial climb quite steep but the slope is also south facing, requiring an early start on sunny and hot days in order to beat the heat.

KID TIP I The steep and sometimes rough trail makes this trip ill suited for small children.

TRAILHEAD I 39°11.396'N, 119°47.634'W From North Carson Street, turn west onto West College Parkway and travel 0.7 mile to a right turn onto North Ormsby Boulevard. After 0.2 mile, Ormsby turns left and becomes Coombs Canyon Road, which you follow another half mile to a right turn

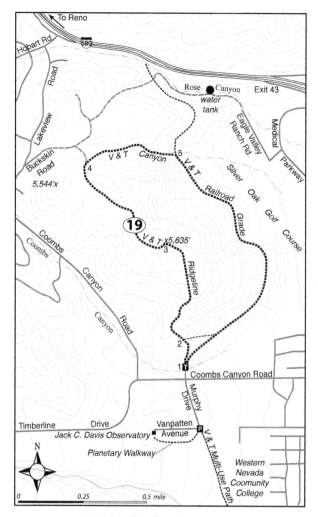

19. V & T Ridgeline–Canyon Loop

onto a dirt road at Murphy Drive. Park your vehicle at the end of the road as space allows.

TRAIL | The route starts climbing steeply right from the start, as you ascend to the north up an open hillside on a single-track path through grassy vegetation and widely scattered sagebrush. Head upslope toward some low rock outcroppings and boulders, while taking the time to catch your breath and enjoy the view across the north end of Eagle Valley to the Pine Nut Mountains in the distance. The trail bends northwest and comes to an unsigned junction **[2]** at 0.1 mile, where a fainter path heads over to connect with the V & T Railroad grade. The trail soon gains the ridge, offering a brief respite from the intense climbing before quickly resuming the ascent up the ridge. Farther upslope the tread becomes rockier, as it weaves through the outcroppings and boulders seen from below. Views improve along the way with the gain in elevation. At around 0.3 mile, the grade gratefully eases on the approach to the high point. The trail eventually leads just past the rock outcrop forming the true summit, requiring a short and easy scramble to reach the 5,635-foot top. [3] As expected, you have a wide-ranging view from this aerie in all directions.

A pleasant stroll leads away from the top and down the ridge to the northwest until the trail makes a sharp bend and descends more steeply to where you merge with a twin-tracked section of old road on the way to a more defined stretch of road. Follow this road generally north, keeping your eyes peeled for an indistinct path marked by a large cairn [4] heading west down a canyon. (If you reach a junction with Buckskin Road, you've traveled about 0.1 mile too far.)

Turn right onto the faint track on an initially gentle descent into the head of the canyon. The trail does become more defined farther down the draw, as the descent gets steeper. Fortunately, the old railroad grade is clearly visible below, so even without the aid of defined trail, you should be able to easily navigate your way down the canyon to the old bed of the V & T Railroad, [5] 1.75 miles from the trailhead.

Turn right onto the railroad grade and follow the gentle course back toward the trailhead. Fine views across the Silver Oak Golf Course and the Carson Tahoe medical campus to McLellan Peak accompany you on the way back. Reach the trailhead at 3.8 miles. [1]

GREAT BASIN RATTLESNAKE (*Crotalus oreganus lutosus*) A sign near the trailhead warns about the presence of rattlesnakes in the area. A subspecies of the western rattlesnake, the brownish-patterned Great Basin rattlesnake reaches one and a half to four feet in length at maturity. They have a triangular head and the characteristic rattle at the tail. Their diet consists primarily of amphibians, reptiles, birds, eggs, and small mammals. Although their bites are poisonous to humans, these snakes are not aggressive and will preferentially flee the presence of humans unless all escape routes are blocked. Their first line of their defense is to remain motionless in hopes their camouflage coloring will keep them from being detected. If humans come too close, they will oftentimes give an audible warning with their rattles. Reserving their venom for prey, rattlesnakes are reluctant to bite humans.

Great Basin Rattlesnake

1: Start at trailhead; **2:** Straight at junction; **3:** Top of Peak 5,365; **4:** Right at junction; **5:** Right at V & T junction; **1:** Return to trailhead.

GO GREEN | Muscle Powered is the preeminent organization for building and maintaining trails in Carson City. Established in 1999, the group has been an unparalleled advocate for biking and hiking trails in the area. Along with trail building and maintenance, education, and advocacy, the nonprofit group also hosts community events. They routinely sponsor trash mobs, cleanup projects that make a valuable contribution to the beautification of the greater Carson City area. You can become a member and support the work at www.musclepowered.org.

OPTIONS | Old roads and unofficial trails crisscross the area and offer options for farther wanderings, although they may be on private property. A recent extension allows a connection to the trails on the Carson Tahoe Medical Center campus (see Trip 10C).

20 | Vicee Canyon Loop

The farther one goes on this trip that begins at the edge of a neighborhood on the west side of town, the greater the feeling of getting away from it all. A steady climb toward the base of the Carson Range is rewarded by improving views of the surrounding terrain, followed by a pleasant descent along the rim of lower Vicee Canyon. While a maze of old roads and paths crisscross the area, the well-defined, single-track tread of the combination of the Jackrabbit, Postal, Seven Steps, and Vicee Canyon Trails should be easy for most recreationists to follow.

LEVEL	Hike, intermediate
LENGTH	3 miles, lollipop loop
TIME	1-1/2 to 2 hours
ELEVATION	+450'/–450'
USERS	Hikers, trail runners, mountain bikers, equestrians
DOGS	OK
DIFFICULTY	Moderate
SEASON	All year
BEST TIME	Spring, fall
FACILITIES	Trash can
MAP	None
MANAGEMENT	Carson City Parks, Recreation, and Open Space at 775-887-2262, www.carson.org/government/departments-g-z/parks-recreation-open-space
HIGHLIGHTS	Creek, scenery
LOWLIGHTS	Exposed to sun—hot in summer

TIP | Since this trip offers no shade, getting an early start on warm and sunny days would be a wise move.

KID TIP | The three-mile length of this trip may be just the right distance for youngsters who have successfully completed shorter trips and are ready to extend their outings on a longer hike. Be sure to pack plenty of sunscreen, water, and maybe a tasty snack as a reward.

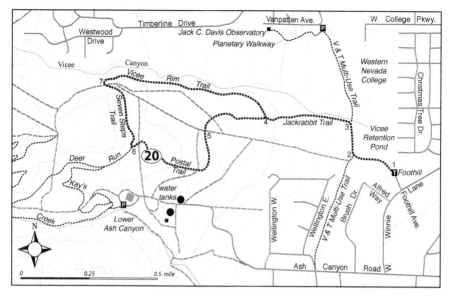

20. Vicee Canyon Loop

TRAILHEAD | 39°10'743'N, 119°47.298'W From North Carson Street, head west on West Winnie Lane and travel 1.1 miles to a right-hand turn onto Foothill Drive. Continue the short distance to the end of Foothill, and park your vehicle on the side of the road as space allows.

TRAIL | Pass around a closed steel gate and follow a single-track trail along a fence line through typical sagebrush scrub vegetation with the massive pit of the Vicee Retention Pond on your right. At the intersection with the paved V & T Multi-Use Trail, [2] turn right (north) and walk about four hundred yards to the starting point of the Jackrabbit Trail [3] on the left, just prior to the crossing of Vicee Canyon creek.

Leaving the pleasant grade of the paved trail, begin climbing west along the south rim of the drainage, passing some retention ponds and a couple of old roads that cross the single-track trail along the way upstream. Continue toward the base of the Carson Range, reaching a Y junction [4] at 0.6 mile from the trailhead, where the continuation of the Jackrabbit Trail veers slightly left and the Vicee Rim Trail angles to the right.

Remaining on the Jackrabbit Trail, proceed ahead to the west for a bit and then follow the trail on a curve to the south, crossing another old road on the way toward a lone Jeffrey pine near the intersection [5] with a well-defined road, where the Jackrabbit Trail becomes the Postal Trail. Traverse ahead to the south for a while before the trail bends around to the west again and resumes a stiffer climb, crossing over another couple of roads on the way to a three-way junction near the base of a hill, 1.4 miles from the trailhead. [6] At the junction, the Deer Run Trail on the left heads southwest, and the Seven Steps Trail on the right goes north.

Turn right and follow the Seven Steps Trail on a descending traverse across the base of the hill past very widely spaced Jeffrey pines, enjoying fine views of Carson City and the surrounding terrain on the way toward Vicee Canyon. Eventually the trail bends northwest and passes above a well-traveled road below. Soon you pass through a copse of taller pines, bend around to cross the road, [7] and then drop shortly to the rim of Vicee Canyon. Initially, houses above the north side of the canyon take away from the undeveloped ambiance of the upper trail. Head downstream along the rim of the canyon on a steady descent, reaching the end of the loop [4] at 2.4 miles. From there, retrace your steps to the trailhead. [1]

BLACK-TAILED JACKRABBIT (*Lepus californicus*) Not in the rabbit but the hare family, these mammals are found in the desert and foothill environments of western Nevada. With their characteristic long ears, which can grow up to eight inches, and their long hind legs with large feet, they are easily distinguished from the smaller cottontail rabbits common to the area. Jackrabbits are most likely to be seen by hikers around dusk, as they emerge from their hollows to forage under the relative safety of low-light conditions.

MILESTONES

1: Start at trailhead; 2: Right at V & T junction; 3: Left at Jackrabbit junction; 4: Slight left at Loop junction; 5: Straight at road junction; 6: Right at Seven Steps / Deer Run junction; 7: Cross road; 4: Left at Loop junction;
1: Return to trailhead.

GO GREEN | Muscle Powered is the preeminent organization for building and maintaining trails in Carson City. Established in 1999, the group has been an unparalleled advocate for biking and hiking trails in the area. Along with trail building and maintenance, education, and advocacy, the nonprofit group also hosts community events. They routinely sponsor trash mobs, cleanup projects that make a valuable contribution to the beautification of the greater Carson City area. You can become a member and support the work at www.musclepowered.org.

OPTIONS | An extensive system of connecting trails makes crafting a longer trip in the area quite easy.

Ash Canyon Creek begins on the east slope of Snow Valley Peak near the crest of the Carson Range and tumbles down the namesake gorge toward Carson City. This trip initially follows the 1.3-mile Creek Trail along a stretch of the stream in the lower canyon through the transition zone between sagebrush scrub and Jeffrey pine forest. Combining the Creek Trail with the Four Day, Baldy Green, Deer Run, and Kay's Trails creates a 3.5-mile loop well suited for a morning or afternoon jaunt.

LEVEL	Hike, intermediate
LENGTH	3.5 miles, loop
TIME	1-1/2 to 2 hours
ELEVATION	+500′/–500′
USERS	Hikers, trail runners, mountain bikers, equestrians
DOGS	OK
DIFFICULTY	Moderate
SEASON	All year
BEST TIMES	Spring, fall
FACILITIES	None
MAP	None
MANAGEMENT	Carson City Parks, Recreation, and Open Space at 775-887-2262, www.carson.org/government/departments-g-z/parks-recreation-open-space
HIGHLIGHTS	Autumn color, creek, views
LOWLIGHTS	Poorly signed

TIP | Drive very slowly up the access road to the water tanks, as you must cross several water bars on the way that could damage your vehicle if you drive too fast.

KID TIP | Children usually find flowing water to be a quite captivating environment, and Ash Canyon Creek should be no exception. By using two vehicles or arranging for a shuttle, you could easily reduce the trip to just the 1.3-mile section along the creek and avoid the extra 2-plus miles across dry slopes that some kids may find less interesting.

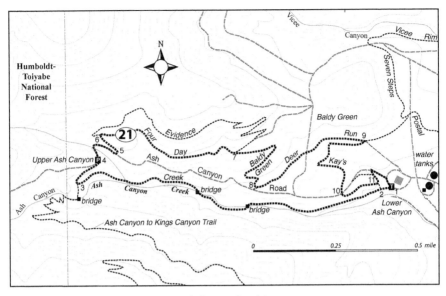

21. Ash Canyon Creek Loop

TRAILHEAD | 39°10.653′N, 119°48.059′W From North Carson Street, drive west on West Winnie Lane for 1.4 miles and turn right onto Ash Canyon Road. Head west on Ash Canyon Road for 0.5 mile to the end of the housing development, where the road bends and makes a winding ascent to the vicinity of a pair of water tanks. At the end of the pavement, continue ahead past the tanks a short distance to a small reservoir, take the left-hand road, and park your vehicle in the wide area near the reservoir's southeast corner.

TRAIL | Finding the start of the unmarked trail is perhaps the most difficult part of this trip, which presents you with a couple of options. The first option involves leaving the immediate vicinity of the parking area on a faint stretch of single-track trail that drops slightly down the hillside and heads south-southwest for a short distance to an informal junction **[2]** with a path connecting to the Ash Canyon Road. The alternative is to simply follow Ash Canyon Road away from the reservoir for about 500 feet to where a single-track trail on the left angles back uphill opposite a sign designating a revegetation area. After a brief climb, this path bends southwest, begins a short descent, reaches a three-way junction, **[10]** and soon comes to the junction with the single-track trail from the reservoir. **[2]**

Travel south-southeast away from the junction and follow a descending traverse across the hillside toward Ash Canyon Creek. Soon you reach the north bank of the stream and head upstream. Gently rising tread leads

Mountain bikers on the Ash Canyon Trail

past cottonwoods, aspens, and willows lining the creek, as widely scattered Jeffrey pines dot the hillside above. At 0.6 mile, the trail bends down and crosses the creek on a two-by-six-plank bridge and then continues along the south bank for 0.2 mile to a second bridge. Proceed upstream through lush riparian vegetation, eventually crossing a bridge over the north branch of Ash Canyon Creek and then reaching a side trail leading over to a small flat with a picnic table next to the water. A short way farther is a signed three-way junction [3] with the Ash to Kings Canyon Trail, 1.3 miles from the trailhead.

Turn right and make a short climb up to the upper Ash Canyon trailhead parking area. [4] From the trailhead, walk down the Ash Canyon Road to a crossing of the north branch of Ash Canyon Creek, and continue along the dirt road for a short way to an unmarked junction [5] with a single-track trail heading up the hillside.

A short climb away from the road leads to the next junction [6] between the Four Day and Evidence Trails. Take the Four Day Trail on your right to head generally eastward on a gently descending traverse across a Jeffrey pine–dotted slope with a light understory of tobacco brush and sagebrush. Keen eyes may detect evidence of a previous fire that swept through this area. Eventually the canyon widens out, which allows good views downslope of Carson City. Reach a junction [7] with the Baldy Green and Evidence Trails at 2.2 miles.

Quaking Aspen leaves

Take the right-hand path, the Baldy Green Trail, and head more steeply downhill across open, grassy slopes to a switchback. The stiff descent continues toward the Ash Canyon Road and a somewhat obscure junction [8] with the Deer Run Trail, which connects very shortly to the road.

Veer to the left away from the road and follow the Deer Run Trail northeast across mostly open slopes. Cross an old jeep road and make a general traverse to the east, reaching a four-way junction at 3 miles. [9] Here the Deer Run Trail continues ahead, Kay's Trail doubles back sharply to the right, and a dirt road heads southeast back toward the reservoir. (This would be the shortest route back to the car.)

Remaining on a single-track trail, turn sharply to the right and follow Kay's Trail back to the west before turning to the south and winding back toward Ash Canyon Road. Cross the road [10] and continue on the trail, which soon bends to the east and proceeds to an unmarked, three-way junction. [11] Turn left and follow the trail back to Ash Canyon Road. From there, simply follow the road back to the parking area by the reservoir. [1]

> **QUAKING ASPEN** (*Populus tremuloides*) Perhaps no autumn sight in the eastern Sierra is more scintillating than a canyon filled with a stand of quaking aspen, when the yellow-green, spade-shaped leaves of summer turn a brilliant orange-gold. Even before they turn, a multitude of leaves trembling in the mildest of breezes can be quite stunning. Although sometimes sprouting from seeds, most aspens sprout from the spreading roots of a single parent, amazingly resulting in stands of genetically identical individuals.

MILESTONES

1: Start at trailhead; **2:** South-southeast from junction; **3:** Right at three-way junction; **4:** Upper Ash Canyon trailhead; **5:** Left at junction; **6:** Right at Evidence junction; **7:** Straight at Baldy Green junction; **8:** Left at Deer Run junction; **9:** Sharp right at Kay's junction; **10:** Cross Ash Canyon Road; **11:** Left at junction; **1:** Return to junction.

GO GREEN | Muscle Powered is the preeminent organization for building and maintaining trails in Carson City. Established in 1999, the group has been an unparalleled advocate for biking and hiking trails in the area. Along with trail building and maintenance, education, and advocacy, the nonprofit group also hosts community events. They routinely sponsor trash mobs, cleanup projects that make a valuable contribution to the beautification of the greater Carson City area. You can become a member and support the work at www.musclepowered.org.

OPTIONS | An extensive system of connecting trails makes crafting a longer trip in the area quite easy.

0   500   1,000 feet

One of Carson City's newest paths, the Overlook Trail was built largely with volunteer labor. The well-built, single-track trail follows a gentle grade geared toward mountain bikers, steadily ascending from the bottom of Ash Canyon up its south wall and then around the foothills of the Carson Range to a viewpoint on top of a rock outcrop. Passing through mostly open terrain, the route offers grand views along the way as well as from the overlook.

LEVEL	Hike, intermediate
LENGTH	5.8 miles, out and back
TIME	2 to 3 hours
ELEVATION	+625'/–150'
USERS	Hikers, trail runners, mountain bikers, equestrians
DOGS	OK
DIFFICULTY	Moderate
SEASON	Spring through fall
BEST TIMES	Late spring to early summer, fall
FACILITIES	None
MAP	Carson City: *Ash to Kings Trail* (carson.org/home /showdocument?id=52881)
MANAGEMENT	Carson City Parks, Recreation, and Open Space at 775-887-2262, www.carson.org/government/departments-g-z/parks -recreation-open-space
HIGHLIGHTS	Canyon, creek, views
LOWLIGHTS	None

TIP I Drive very slowly up the access road to the water tanks, as you must cross several water bars on the way that could damage your vehicle if you drive too fast.

KID TIP I Graded primarily for the benefit of mountain bikers, without any steep climbing, the Overlook Trail should be fairly easily managed by all but the smallest of children. As the trail is popular with the two-wheeled crowd, make sure your youngsters are well versed in trail etiquette.

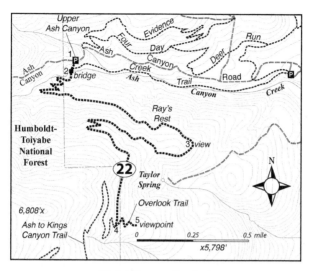

22. Ash Canyon Overlook

TRAILHEAD | 39°10.698′N, 119°49.405′W From North Carson Street, drive west on West Winnie Lane for 1.4 miles and turn right onto Ash Canyon Road. Head west on Ash Canyon Road for 0.5 mile to the end of the housing development, where the road bends and makes a winding ascent to the vicinity of a pair of water tanks. At the end of the pavement, continue ahead past the tanks a short distance to a small reservoir, and continue up the dirt road another mile to the parking area for the upper Ash Canyon trailhead.

TRAIL | From the trailhead, follow a single-track trail down to a three-way junction [2] with the Creek Trail on your left, and continue a short distance to a wood-rail bridge across willow- and alder-lined Ash Canyon Creek. Beyond the bridge, the steady, well-graded climb to the overlook begins, soon switchbacking up the north-facing slope of Ash Canyon. Above the fifth switchback, the trail follows a lengthy, gently rising traverse headed generally southeast past Ray's Rest to the nose of the ridge [3] and marvelous sweeping views to the north and east, 1.5 miles from the trailhead. The nice views make this location a satisfactory turnaround point if you're interested in a shorter trip.

From the viewpoint, the trail continues its gradual ascent, doubling back for a stretch before a set of switchbacks leads up the hillside and around the nose of the next ridge across mostly open slopes carpeted with tobacco brush. Here you have some more grand views, extending from McClellan Peak above the north end of Eagle Valley all the way south to the Pine Nut Mountains. From the viewpoint, a long, upward traverse heads south across the hillside to a Y junction, [4] 2.8 miles from the trailhead.

View from the Ash Canyon Overlook Trail

Ash Canyon Creek

Turn left at the junction and follow a winding descent to the overlook [5] perched on a rock outcrop. After thoroughly enjoying the vista, retrace your steps to the trailhead. [1]

> **ASH CANYON** The Ash Canyon watershed is a critical contributor to the municipal water supply of Carson City. Water is diverted near the mouth of the canyon and then piped to the Quill Water Treatment Plant, where it is processed and then delivered to the taps of residents and businesses across Carson City. In addition to Ash Canyon Creek, the plant treats water from Kings Canyon Creek and Marlette Lake. "Leave no trace" principles should always be practiced while recreating near any water source.

MILESTONES

1: Start at trailhead; 2: Straight at junction; 3: View; 4: Left at Y junction; 5: Overlook; 1: Return to trailhead.

GO GREEN | Muscle Powered is the preeminent organization for building and maintaining trails in Carson City. Established in 1999, the group has been an unparalleled advocate for biking and hiking trails in the area. Along with trail building and maintenance, education, and advocacy, the nonprofit group also hosts community events. They routinely sponsor trash mobs, cleanup projects that make a valuable contribution to the beautification of the greater Carson City area. You can become a member and support the work at www.musclepowered.org.

OPTIONS | With two vehicles or shuttle arrangements, you could opt for the longer route between Ash and Kings Canyons as described in the next trip.

23 | Ash to Kings Trail

The Ash to Kings Trail is one of the premier recreational trails in the Carson City area, especially for mountain bikers, who find the continuously gently graded route between the two canyons to be well suited for their activity. The two-legged crowd should find the gentle nature of the route quite enjoyable as well, which climbs steadily from the upper Ash Canyon trailhead for the first 5 miles before descending just as gradually for 2.5 miles to the end at the upper Kings Canyon trailhead. Along the way are numerous views, pockets of Jeffrey pine forest, and delightful stream canyons.

LEVEL	Hike, intermediate
LENGTH	7.5 miles, shuttle
TIME	1/2 day
ELEVATION	+1,250'/−775'
USERS	Hikers, trail runners, mountain bikers, equestrians
DOGS	OK
DIFFICULTY	Moderate
SEASON	Spring through fall
BEST TIME	Late spring to early summer, fall
FACILITIES	None
MAP	Carson City: *Ash to Kings Trail* (carson.org/home /showdocument?id=52881)
MANAGEMENT	Carson City Parks, Recreation, and Open Space at 775-887-2262, www.carson.org/government/departments-g-z/parks -recreation-open-space
HIGHLIGHTS	Canyon, creeks, forest, views
LOWLIGHTS	Rough access road

TIP | Drive very slowly up the Ash Canyon access road to the water tanks, as you must cross several water bars on the way that could damage your vehicle if you drive too fast. *Note: The Kings Canyon Road beyond the waterfall trailhead received considerable damage in the 2016–2017 winter, which makes getting to the upper trailhead a challenge even for 4WD vehicles. Check with Carson*

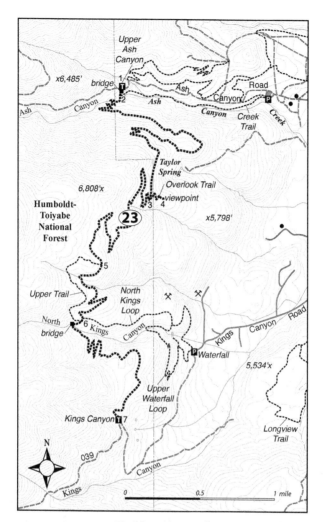

23. Ash to Kings Trail

City Parks, Recreation, and Open Space or the Carson Ranger District about current conditions.

KID TIP | Even though the entire trail is well graded without any steep climbs, the 7.5-mile distance is probably a bit much for younger children.

TRAILHEAD START | 39°10.698'N, 119°49.405'W From North Carson Street, drive west on West Winnie Lane for 1.4 miles and turn right onto Ash Canyon Road. Head west on Ash Canyon Road for 0.5 mile to the end of the housing development, where the road bends and makes a winding ascent to

Hikers enjoying the view of Eagle Valley from the trail

the vicinity of a pair of water tanks. At the end of the pavement, continue ahead past the tanks a short distance to a small reservoir and continue up the dirt road another mile to the parking area for the upper Ash Canyon trailhead.

END | 39°09.211′N, 119°48.932′W From the vicinity of the capitol building in downtown Carson City, travel south on Carson Street for one block and turn right (west) onto West 2nd Street. After one block, turn right (north) onto South Curry Street, go another block, and then turn left (west) onto West King Street. Follow the road out of town, where it becomes Kings Canyon Road, and continue to the end of the pavement, about 3 miles from downtown. Park your vehicle near the marked trailhead along the shoulder of the road as space allows.

TRAIL | From the trailhead, follow a single-track trail down to a three-way junction [2] with the Creek Trail on your left, and continue a short distance to a wood-rail bridge across willow- and alder-lined Ash Canyon Creek. Beyond the bridge, the steady, well-graded climb to the overlook begins, soon switchbacking up the north-facing slope of Ash Canyon. Above the fifth switchback, the trail follows a lengthy, gently rising traverse headed generally southeast past Ray's Rest to the nose of the ridge [3] and marvelous sweeping views to the north and east, 1.5 miles from the trailhead. The nice views make this location a satisfactory turnaround point if you're interested in a shorter trip.

The Ash to Kings Trail offers many outstanding vistas

From the viewpoint, the trail continues its gradual ascent, doubling back for a stretch before a set of switchbacks leads up the hillside and around the nose of the next ridge across mostly open slopes carpeted with tobacco brush. Here you have some more grand views, extending from McClellan Peak above the north end of Eagle Valley all the way south to the Pine Nut Mountains. From the viewpoint, a long, upward traverse heads south across the hillside to a Y junction, [4] 2.8 miles from the trailhead.

Turn left at the junction and follow a winding descent to the overlook [5] perched on a rock outcrop. After thoroughly enjoying the vista, retrace your steps to the junction. [4]

From the overlook junction, continue southbound for a short while to a pair of switchbacks, followed by a longer ascent toward the canyon of a seasonal stream. Here, a pair of long-legged switchbacks climbs away from the canyon before traversing above it through an old burn area. A long steady climb leads around the nose of another ridge, and then two more long-legged switchbacks take you higher up the slope and into Jeffrey pine forest. More climbing leads to the high point of the trip just below 6,700 feet and a junction [6] a short way farther with the Upper Trail, 5.1 miles from the trailhead.

Over the next mile, you make a steady descent following the folds and creases of the topography around a seasonal stream canyon. Beyond the stream, switchbacks lead out of the forest and back onto open slopes on the way to a four-way junction [7] with an old road, 6.1 miles from the trailhead. Here the combined route of the Ash to Kings Trail and the Upper Waterfall Loop veers ahead to the left and resumes on single track. The uphill road continues higher up into the Carson Range, while the downhill section is part of the Upper Waterfall Loop, which heads back to the Waterfall trailhead. *Note: if you were unable to get a vehicle up to the upper Kings Canyon trailhead and left a car at the Waterfall trailhead, you may want to consider taking the Upper Waterfall Loop trail down to the trailhead to avoid the long walk on the Kings Canyon Road.*

From the junction, follow the single-track trail through a scattered forest of Jeffrey pines on a gentle descent leading to a crossing of the stream flowing through North Kings Canyon on a wood-railed bridge. From the creek, the trail turns down canyon and exits the forest on the way to a set of switchbacks zigzagging down the open hillside. At the bottom of the descent, you hop across the southern branch of the creek. Away from the stream, a mellow stretch of trail travels in and out of Jeffrey pine forest on the way around point 6256, followed by a southerly traverse toward a union with the Kings Canyon Road. Shortly before reaching the road near a hairpin turn, you bend into the gully of a seasonal stream and then drop to the junction [8] at the upper Kings Canyon Road trailhead. If you have a vehicle waiting for you at the upper trailhead, your trip is over. Otherwise, you must walk another 1.4 miles along the Ash Canyon Road to reach the Waterfall trailhead. [9]

JEFFREY PINE (*Pinus jeffreyi*) The ubiquitous Jeffrey pine is a common sight at these elevations in the east front of the Carson Range. One of two three-needled pines found in the Sierra, Jeffrey pines differ from their ponderosa pine counterparts, with larger cones and reddish-brown bark that often emits a vanilla scent. Ponderosa pines generally prefer wetter soils than Jeffreys, which is why Jeffrey pines are typically more common on the drier east side of the range.

Jeffrey Pine branch and cone

MILESTONES

1: Start at trailhead; **2:** Straight at junction; **3:** View; **4:** Left at Y junction; **5:** Overlook; **6:** Straight at Upper Trail junction; **7:** Ahead, left at road junction; **8:** Upper Kings Canyon trailhead; **9:** Waterfall trailhead.

GO GREEN | Muscle Powered is the preeminent organization for building and maintaining trails in Carson City. Established in 1999, the group has been an unparalleled advocate for biking and hiking trails in the area. Along with trail building and maintenance, education, and advocacy, the nonprofit group also hosts community events. They routinely sponsor trash mobs, cleanup projects that make a valuable contribution to the beautification of the greater Carson City area. You can become a member and support the work at www.musclepowered.org.

OPTIONS | A proposal is in the works for the Capital to Lake Tahoe Nevada State Park Trail, a 7-mile extension from the upper part of the Ash to Kings Trail. As mentioned, if accessing the upper Kings Canyon trailhead is impossible due to rough road conditions, leaving a second vehicle at the Waterfall trailhead would allow you to descend the north part of the Upper Waterfall Loop, thereby avoiding the 1.4-mile, somewhat tedious descent along the Kings Canyon Road back to the trailhead.

Waterfall Trail and North Kings Canyon Loop

Recent improvements to the trail network in the Kings Canyon area have created an enjoyable number of options for hikes of varying lengths and ranges of difficulty. The short out-and-back trip to the waterfall on the creek spilling down North Kings Canyon is easy enough for just about anyone. The longer option on the North Kings Canyon Loop offers a nearly two-mile extension, with views of the surrounding countryside, as well as a bird's-eye glimpse of the waterfall from the top of the canyon.

LEVEL	Hike, intermediate (beginner to waterfall only)
LENGTH	1.8 miles, loop (0.6 mile, out and back to waterfall only)
TIME	1 hour
ELEVATION	+500'/–500'
USERS	Hikers, trail runners
DOGS	OK
DIFFICULTY	Moderate
SEASON	Spring through fall
BEST TIME	Late April to late May
FACILITIES	None
MAP	Carson City: *Ash to Kings Trail* (carson.org/home/showdocument?id=52881)
MANAGEMENT	Carson City Parks, Recreation, and Open Space at 775-887-2262, www.carson.org/government/departments-g-z/parks-recreation-open-space; Humboldt-Toiyabe National Forest, Carson Ranger District at 775-882-2766, www.fs.usda.gov/htnf
HIGHLIGHTS	Stream, views, waterfall
LOWLIGHTS	Exposed to sun—hot in summer.

TIP | The waterfall is fullest when spring snowmelt is underway, usually late April through May. Summer temperatures can be quite hot away from the cool spray of the fall, so get an early start if you plan your hike during the warmer months of the year.

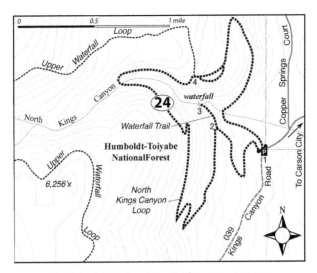

24. Waterfall Trail and North Kings Canyon Loop

KID TIP ǀ Moving water seems to captivate most children, with the full loop offering not only an up-close look at the waterfall but also a downstream crossing of the creek.

TRAILHEAD ǀ 39°09.211′N, 119°48.932′W From the vicinity of the capitol building in downtown Carson City, travel south on Carson Street for one block and turn right (west) onto West 2nd Street. After one block, turn right (north) onto South Curry Street, go another block, and then turn left (west) onto West King Street. Follow the road out of town, where it becomes Kings Canyon Road, and continue to the end of the pavement, about 3 miles from downtown. Park your vehicle near the marked trailhead along the shoulder of the road as space allows.

TRAIL ǀ With the continuation of the dirt section of Kings Canyon Road to the left and an unmarked, gated dirt road to the right, head up a set of stairs for the marked Waterfall Trail past a trailhead kiosk onto single-track tread through typical scrub vegetation. Unfortunately, some shortcut paths make discerning the established trail a bit difficult, but follow the lower option headed south across the hillside to a switchback, and then angle generally north on a moderate climb with fine views to the east. Soon you reach a three-way junction, [2] where the trail to the waterfall proceeds ahead and the North Kings Canyon Loop is to the left.

Continue ahead, as the Waterfall Trail bends into the canyon, passes a berm on the uphill side, and then soon reaches the waterfall [3] cascading down a near vertical wall of dark rock. After enjoying this little oasis, return the short distance to the junction. [2]

A photographer captures a shot of the waterfall

Big Sagebrush

If you're only interested in the trip to the waterfall and back, retrace your steps to the trailhead. [1] Otherwise, veer to the right and follow the North Kings Canyon Loop on a southward traverse before gently rising tread leads to a switchback. A stiffer climb leads up the hillside via a pair of short-legged switchbacks before another section of rising traverse heads north, crossing onto US Forest Service (USFS) land along the way. Just beyond the top of a rock outcrop, you follow another pair of short-legged switchbacks up the hillside and then bend northwest into North Kings Canyon. After a brief drop to the creek, follow a bridge to the far bank, and then head down the canyon before the trail gently climbs away from the stream and a level stretch leads to a marked junction with a dirt road that serves as a connector to the Ash to Kings Trail. [4]

Proceed to the right and follow the dirt road, soon reaching a side trail on the right that bends to the edge of the bluff to allow a bird's-eye view of the waterfall in the canyon below before shortly rejoining the road. From there, the road descends stiffly north to a hairpin turn, where the road then follows a descending arc back to a crossing of the creek and then down to the close of the loop at the trailhead. [1]

> **BIG SAGEBRUSH** (*Artemesia tridentata*) No other plant is more associated with the Great Basin than the big sagebrush, which carpets the foothills of the vast number of mountain ranges within Nevada. This gray-green shrub produces small yellow flowers (Nevada's state flower) that appear in late summer or early fall. The average height of the plant is two to four feet. Perhaps the most notable aspect of the plant is the pungent fragrance it emits, particularly after a rain shower.

MILESTONES

1: Start at trailhead; 2: Straight at Waterfall junction; 3: Waterfall; 2: Veer right at Waterfall junction; 4: Straight at road junction; 1: Return to trailhead.

GO GREEN | Muscle Powered is the preeminent organization for building and maintaining trails in Carson City. Established in 1999, the group has been an unparalleled advocate for biking and hiking trails in the area. Along with trail building and maintenance, education, and advocacy, the nonprofit group also hosts community events. They routinely sponsor trash mobs, cleanup projects that make a valuable contribution to the beautification of the greater Carson City area. You can become a member and support the work at www.musclepowered.org.

OPTIONS | For a longer trip in the same area, consider the nearly five-mile loop as described in Trip 25.

The Upper Waterfall Loop provides a fine ramble through the western foot-hills above Carson City. The route begins on a stiff climb up a closed jeep road. From there, you wander along recently constructed single track, traveling in and out of Jeffrey pine forest and visiting riparian areas in branches of the creek flowing through North Kings Canyon. The trip concludes by following a section of the multi-use Kings Canyon Road back down to the trailhead.

LEVEL	Intermediate, hike
LENGTH	4.9 miles, loop
TIME	2 to 3 hours
ELEVATION	+1,000'/–1,000'
USERS	Hikers, trail runners, mountain bikers, equestrians
DOGS	OK
DIFFICULTY	Moderate
SEASON	April to November
BEST TIMES	Spring, fall
FACILITIES	None
MAP	Carson City: *Ash to Kings Trail* (carson.org/home /showdocument?id=52881)
MANAGEMENT	Carson City Parks, Recreation, and Open Space at 775-887-2262, www.carson.org/government/departments-g-z/parks -recreation-open-space; Humboldt-Toiyabe National Forest, Carson Ranger District at 775-882-2766, www.fs.usda.gov /htnf
HIGHLIGHTS	Forest, stream, views
LOWLIGHTS	Hot in summer, exposed to sun

TIP | Arrive early in the morning on hot summer days and pack plenty of sunscreen and water.

KID TIP | Smaller children are probably better served by the shorter North Canyon Loop, which is closed to vehicles, bicycles, and horses.

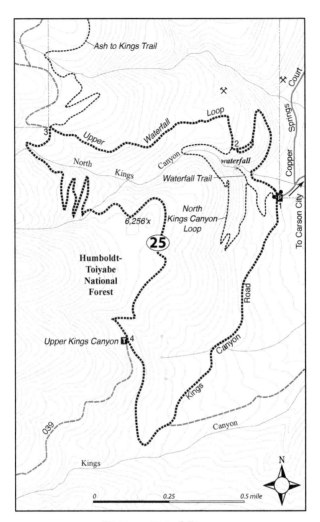

25. Upper Waterfall Loop

TRAILHEAD | 39°09.211'N, 119°48.932'W From the vicinity of the capitol building in downtown Carson City, travel south on Carson Street for one block and turn right (west) onto West 2nd Street. After one block, turn right (north) onto South Curry Street, go another block, and then turn left (west) onto West King Street. Follow the road out of town, where it becomes Kings Canyon Road, and continue to the end of the pavement, about 3 miles from downtown. Park your vehicle near the marked trailhead along the shoulder of the road as space allows.

TRAIL | From the vicinity of the trailhead, follow the gated road to the north and make a moderate to moderately steep climb up a hillside carpeted with scrub vegetation that bends into North Fork Kings Canyon and crosses the stream on a wood bridge. Continue the ascent across open slopes to a hairpin turn and then up to the top of a rise. Here, a use trail on the left wanders over to the edge of the canyon for a bird's-eye view of the waterfall below and then shortly rejoins the road. After a short distance, you reach a three-way junction [2] with the North Kings Canyon Loop.

From the junction, continue on the road bending uphill to the right on a stiff climb before the grade moderates temporarily. Here you have fine views of the western foothills above Eagle Valley and east out to the Pine Nut Mountains. The steep ascent resumes near the USFS boundary on the way to the top of a rise and a signed, four-way junction. [3]

From the junction, follow a single-track trail through a scattered forest of Jeffrey pines on a gentle descent leading to a crossing of the stream flowing through North Kings Canyon on a wood-railed bridge. From the creek, the trail turns down canyon and exits the forest on the way to a set of switchbacks zigzagging down the open hillside. At the bottom of the descent, you hop across the southern branch of the creek. Away from the stream, a mellow stretch of trail travels in and out of Jeffrey pine forest on the way around point 6256, followed by a southerly traverse toward a union with the Kings Canyon Road. Shortly before reaching the road near a hairpin turn, you bend into the gully of a seasonal stream and then drop to the junction [4] at the upper Kings Canyon Road trailhead.

Turn downhill and head generally south on the sometimes rocky and dusty road on a moderate 1.4-mile descent toward Kings Canyon. Just before reaching the canyon, the road bends northeast and continues the descent back to the Waterfall trailhead. [1]

KINGS CANYON ROAD What is now a favorite of the 4WD crowd was once the principal route that connected the mines of the Comstock Lode to Placerville, California. Following an original Washoe Indian trail, the path saw an increase in use by would-be miners hoping to strike it rich in the California gold rush. As settlement around Carson City increased, Nevada's territorial government approved construction of a road through Kings Canyon to Spooner's Station (near Glenbrook) in 1862, which was completed in November of the following year. This thoroughfare became the preferred way to travel between Carson City and Lake Tahoe for many years and saw little change until the advent of the automobile. Improvement to the road started in 1914, which eventually became part of the state's highway system. The road's heyday

A mountain biker takes a picture from the Kings Canyon Road

lasted for another fourteen years until a more modern paved highway through Clear Creek Canyon was built in 1928, which ultimately became US 50. Kings Canyon Road was eventually removed from the state highway system in 2010.

MILESTONES

1: Start at trailhead; **2:** Right at North Kings Canyon Loop junction; **3:** Left at junction; **4:** Left at Kings Canyon Road junction; **1:** Return to trailhead.

GO GREEN | Muscle Powered is the preeminent organization for building and maintaining trails in Carson City. Established in 1999, the group has been an unparalleled advocate for biking and hiking trails in the area. Along with trail building and maintenance, education, and advocacy, the nonprofit group also hosts community events. They routinely sponsor trash mobs, cleanup projects that make a valuable contribution to the beautification of the greater Carson City area. You can become a member and support the work at www.musclepowered.org.

OPTIONS | If you're not too tuckered out after the nearly five-mile hike, you may want to consider taking the short hike to the base of the waterfall, particularly if your visit is in the spring months when the fall is running full.

26 | C Hill

The prominent hill with the big letter *C* above the southwest part of town is an iconic Carson City landmark that not only identifies the locality but also, for some, issues a siren call to scale its summit. The distance may be short, but the way is steep, and the path is certainly far from the best-constructed trail in the area. For those who don't mind these challenges, the climb can be invigorating, and the view from the top is a more-than-worthy reward for all the effort.

LEVEL	Hike, advanced
LENGTH	1.75 miles, lollipop loop
TIME	1 hour
ELEVATION	+950'/−950'
USERS	Hikers, trail runners
DOGS	OK
DIFFICULTY	Strenuous
SEASON	All year
BEST TIMES	Spring, fall
FACILITIES	Trash can
MAP	None
MANAGEMENT	Carson City Parks, Recreation, and Open Space at 775-887-2262, www.carson.org/government/departments-g-z/parks-recreation-open-space; Humboldt-Toiyabe National Forest, Carson Ranger District at 775-882-2766, www.fs.usda.gov/htnf
HIGHLIGHTS	Summit, views
LOWLIGHTS	Numerous side trails, poorly marked, poor tread, steep

TIP | Although relatively short, this trail is steep. Get an early start if you plan on hiking when the temperatures are forecasted to be high.

KID TIP | Teens might be up to the task of scaling C Hill, but taking younger kids along on this grueling hike is probably a prescription for trouble.

TRAILHEAD | 39°09.567′N, 119°46.852′W From South Carson Street, head west on West 5th Street for 0.6 mile to where the road bends to the south

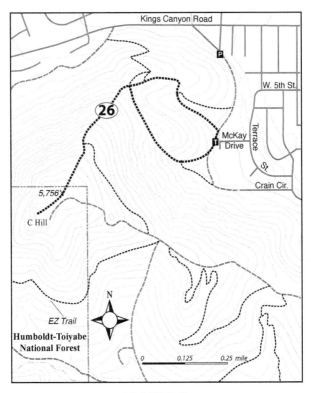

26. C Hill Trails

and becomes Terrace Street. After 0.2 mile, turn right onto McKay Drive and drive the short distance to the end of the road and a dirt parking area opposite the entrance to a Church of Jesus Christ of Latter-day Saints church. Park your vehicle as space allows.

TRAIL | From the parking area, walk up the hill to access an old dirt road. **[2]** Turn left and follow this road on an upward traverse for about three hundred feet to a junction **[3]** with a single-track trail on the right headed more steeply up the slope. Follow the single-track trail up a hillside carpeted with typical sagebrush scrub vegetation, including an abundance of cheat grass. Just past a rock outcrop, the grade eases for a stretch on the way to a four-way junction **[4]** where you gain the northeast ridge of C Hill, about half a mile from the trailhead. (Ignore the crossing of a faint trail a short way prior to the ridge.)

Turn left and climb steeply uphill on sometimes poor tread, which offers improving views of the surrounding terrain with the gain in elevation. After 0.2 mile, you intersect a trail **[5]** on the left that heads southeast and

A view of C Hill

connects with a 4WD road, which provides a connection to the EZ Trail. Continue ahead on the stiff climb toward the summit of C Hill, passing a cluster of boulders on the way. Nearing the top, another path comes in from the left that connects shortly to the 4WD Road. A brief ascent from there leads to the 5,756-foot northeast summit. The slightly higher southwest summit is just a short walk away and offers a sweeping view from the north end of Eagle Valley down the plain of Carson Valley to distant peaks near the south end of the Carson Range. A long stretch of the Pine Nut Mountains is seen to the east. After a sufficient time to absorb the views, retrace your steps to the junction. [4]

You could simply return directly to the trailhead [1] or add a little variety to the trip by taking the north loop back. From the four-way junction, [4] go straight and follow gently descending single-track tread to the east for a short way toward a low rock outcrop. Before reaching the outcrop, at an unmarked junction [6] follow a trail that bends to the right and drops into a draw and heads southeast toward the road at the base of the hill. Once at the road, walk the short distance back to the trailhead parking area. [1]

KIT CARSON (1809–1868) Christopher "Kit" Carson's name is not only affixed to Nevada's state capital but also to a host of other western geographic features. Born in Kentucky, Carson made his way west to Santa Fe, New Mexico, as a teenager, working as a cook, interpreter, and miner before setting off for California in 1829 with some trappers. Returning to New Mexico, he joined up with Thomas Fitzpatrick and spent the next decade trapping in the Rocky Mountains, gaining all the experience he would need to become a well-respected guide. In 1842 he was tabbed by John C. Fremont to be the expedition guide to the Wind River Range in Wyoming. His competence allowed Carson to be Fremont's guide over the next several years on three expeditions through California and Oregon. As the United States had an insatiable appetite for tales from the West, Fremont's expedition reports became the stuff of legend, as did Kit Carson's contributions. Carson will be forever linked to the images of the wild frontier and westward expansion. William M. Ormsby affixed Carson's name to what would become the Silver State's capital in 1858.

MILESTONES

1: Start at trailhead; **2:** Left at road; **3:** Right at junction of a single-track trail; **4:** Left at junction; **5:** Straight at trail; **4:** Straight at junction; **6:** Right at junction; **1:** Return to trailhead.

GO GREEN | Muscle Powered is the preeminent organization for building and maintaining trails in Carson City. Established in 1999, the group has been an unparalleled advocate for biking and hiking trails in the area. Along with trail building and maintenance, education, and advocacy, the nonprofit group also hosts community events. They routinely sponsor trash mobs, cleanup projects that make a valuable contribution to the beautification of the greater Carson City area. You can become a member and support the work at www.musclepowered.org.

OPTIONS | The Longview Trail (Trip 27) is close by. Although not described in this guide, you can easily connect with the EZ Trail, which can be accessed from a trailhead on Curry Street.

A sometimes steep ascent across the back side of C Hill leads to a sense of remoteness and fine views from the top of a plateau-like expanse.

LEVEL	Hike, intermediate
LENGTH	3.6 miles, lollipop loop
TIME	2 hours
ELEVATION	+750'/−750'
USERS	Hikers, trail runners, mountain bikers, equestrians
DOGS	OK
DIFFICULTY	Moderate
SEASON	All year
BEST TIMES	Spring, fall
FACILITIES	None
MAP	Carson City: *Carson City Multi-Use Routes Map*, 4th ed.
MANAGEMENT	Carson City Parks, Recreation, and Open Space at 775-887-2262, www.carson.org/government/departments-g-z/parks-recreation-open-space; Humboldt-Toiyabe National Forest, Carson Ranger District at 775-882-2766, www.fs.usda.gov/htnf
HIGHLIGHTS	Views
LOWLIGHTS	Poor tread

TIP | Get an early start to beat the heat.

KID TIP | Little ones may find the initial climb to be quite tedious and not particularly enjoyable.

TRAILHEAD | 39°09.739′N, 119°47.612′W From South Carson Street, turn west onto West 5th Street and drive 0.6 mile to a right-hand turn onto Tacoma Avenue. After 0.2 mile, turn left onto West Kings Street and travel another 0.8 mile, as the road becomes Kings Canyon Road, to the trailhead on the left-hand side of the road immediately past the Longview Way–Kingsview Way intersection. Park your vehicle on the narrow dirt shoulder on the south side of Kings Canyon Road.

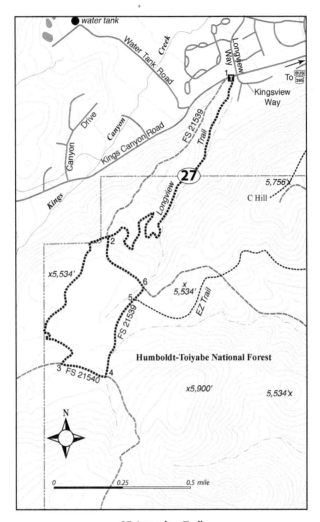

27. Longview Trail

TRAIL | Ignore USFS Road 21539 angling up the hillside and instead follow a narrower road heading up the usually dry drainage to the left of the USFS road. (A sign banning motorized vehicles is placed right at the start.) Head up the drainage through rabbitbrush, sagebrush, and grasses across the northeast flank of C Hill. Where the road curves to the west around the housing development, you continue up the drainage on single-track tread. Farther up, the trail crosses to the west side of the swale and continues a moderate climb for a while before crossing back over to the east side. As you climb, the deepening, V-shaped canyon blocks some of the surrounding development from view, which fosters a wilder feel to the trip. After crossing the drainage one more time, the canyon divides into two channels and you follow the trail up the right-hand (west) branch. After switchbacking, your trail winds up the slope west of the ravine and climbs moderately steeply via more switchbacks with nice views of the surrounding terrain. Pass by an old mine site surrounded by barbed wire and continue to the crest of the hill and a crossing of USFS Road 21539 [2] at 1.2 miles.

Easier hiking leads across the top of the hill, as you head generally southwest while enjoying the views of Borda Meadows and the hills of the Carson Range. After 0.8 mile of pleasant, slightly rising tread, you intersect USFS Road 21540, [3] marked by a cairn.

Turn left (south-southeast) and follow the rocky road for almost 0.2 mile to a T junction [4] with USFS Road 21539.

Turn left again at the junction and travel north-northeast on the gently descending roadbed, passing by a junction [5] with the EZ Trail heading to the east at 2.3 miles. Continue ahead a short way to the next road junction [6] with USFS Road 21539.

Turn left once more and follow Road 21539 over a low rise and down to close the loop at 2.75 miles. From there, retrace your steps down the drainage to the trailhead. [1]

CHEATGRASS (*Bromus tectorum*) For much of northern Nevada, the dominant vegetation carpeting the slopes of the hills is cheatgrass, a nonnative plant originally from the Eurasian steppe. Overgrazing by sheep and cattle during the nineteenth century set the stage for this invasive species to take hold and expand, displacing much of the native sagebrush-grassland vegetation. One unfortunate consequence of this plant invasion is the highly flammable nature of dried cheatgrass contributing to an increase in rangeland fires. Because the seeds of cheatgrass germinate in autumn or early winter, the plant grows more quickly than native species and dries out and burns before the native vegetation has a chance to produce seeds, allowing cheatgrass to become more dominant with each passing season. Complicating matters even further, cheatgrass is nearly impossible to eradicate.

MILESTONES

1: Start at trailhead; 2: Cross USFS Road 21539; 3: Left at junction; 4: Left at junction; 5: Left at junction; 6: Left at junction; 1: Return to trailhead.

GO GREEN ⏐ Muscle Powered is the preeminent organization for building and maintaining trails in Carson City. Established in 1999, the group has been an unparalleled advocate for biking and hiking trails in the area. Along with trail

Cheatgrass

building and maintenance, education, and advocacy, the nonprofit group also hosts community events. They routinely sponsor trash mobs, cleanup projects that provide a valuable asset to the beautification of the greater Carson City area. You can become a member and support the work at www .musclepowered.org.

OPTIONS USFS roads in the area allow you to extend your wanderings farther afield if you so desire.

Clear Creek Trail to Knob Point

One would have to walk a long, long way on the Clear Creek Trail to actually get to the namesake creek, but a couple of viewpoints en route are well worth the time and trouble to get there. The trail begins on the floor of Jacks Valley and utilizes a combination of easy traverses and stiff climbs to gain the necessary elevation to penetrate the east flank of the Carson Range. The route to the first viewpoint at 2 miles remains in the sagebrush scrub zone, while the seven-mile-long trip to the vista at Knob Point eventually enters shady Jeffrey pine forest. Both routes suffer from a lack of water, so make sure you pack plenty, especially if high temperatures are forecast.

LEVEL	Hike, advanced
LENGTH	14 miles, out and back
TIME	Full day
ELEVATION	+1,075'/−100'
USERS	Hikers, trail runners, mountain bikers, equestrians
DOGS	OK
DIFFICULTY	Moderate to strenuous
SEASON	Spring through fall
BEST TIMES	May to June, October
FACILITIES	None
MAP	USGS: *Genoa* (trail not shown); Carson Valley Trails Association: (*Clear Creek Trail*, carsonvalleytrails.org/wp-content/uploads/2016/09/ClearCreekTrailMap.pdf)
MANAGEMENT	Humboldt-Toiyabe National Forest, Carson Ranger District at 775-882-2766, www.fs.usda.gov/htnf
HIGHLIGHTS	Forest, scenery, views
LOWLIGHTS	Lower trail hot in summer—exposed to sun, no water

TIP | As a good portion of the middle part of the trail crosses private property, please respect the rights of these owners by staying on the trail at all times and practicing good trail etiquette.

KID TIP | The overall length of the trip and lack of features on the lower part of the trail probably make this outing ill suited for young children.

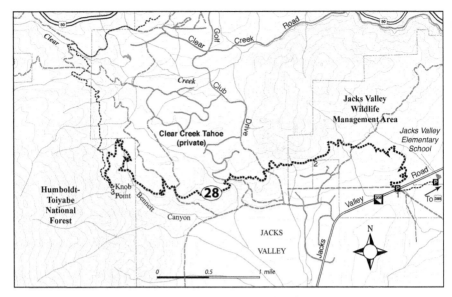

28. Clear Creek Trail to Knob Point

TRAILHEAD | 39°05.509′N, 119°48.347′W Follow South Carson Street to the I-580/US 50 interchange and proceed southbound on US 395 for 1.3 miles to a right-hand turn onto Jacks Valley Road. Drive past Jacks Valley Elementary School to the Clear Creek trailhead on the right side of the road, 1.8 miles from US 395.

TRAIL | From the trailhead parking area, the Clear Creek Trail briefly follows the track of an old road before signage directs you onto the surface of a single-track trail. Make a continual, serpentine ascent to the north through typical sagebrush scrub vegetation on the way past a water tank to the top of the hill, where the path bends to the west and crosses several old jeep roads. Fortunately, trail signs have been placed at these crossings to help keep you on the right track. About 1.5 miles into the trek, a cluster of interesting-looking rock outcrops add some character to the scenery, as the route bends into a pair of usually dry side ravines. Near the 2-mile mark, you reach a prominent rock outcrop [2] offering a good place to rest and take in a fine view of the surrounding valleys bordered to the east by the Pine Nut Mountains. This spot would be an excellent turnaround point for a shorter trip.

To continue, follow the trail on a traverse across the hillside, exiting the Jacks Valley Wildlife Management Area and proceeding onto private property around 2.5 miles from the trailhead. Around this point, you should start to notice the transition from sagebrush scrub to Jeffrey pine forest. As the traverse continues, the trail dips into the forested side canyon of an

Mountain biker on the Clear Creek Trail

intermittent creek, where early-season hikers may find a water source. After crossing the creek on a wood bridge, a stiffer ascent heads up the slope and switchbacks a few times on the way into Bennett Canyon. Climb up the east rim of the canyon for a spell until the trail bends over to cross the usually dry creek bed and then swings around to the south. After about 0.75 mile, you reach a junction where a short stretch of trail leads over to Knob Point. [3] The 6,050-foot vista point rewards you with excellent views across Jacks and Carson Valleys to the Pine Nut Mountains. When the time comes, retrace your steps to the trailhead. [1]

STELLER'S JAY (*Cyanocitta stelleri*) One can't travel for very long through the forests of the Carson Range without seeing one of these blue-and-black jays hopping along the forest floor or hearing its harsh cackle. These jays are also capable of imitating the screams of hawks, so oftentimes visual recognition is necessary to identify between the two. Away from their nest, these jays can be quite noisy, and they can become very bold when accustomed to humans.

MILESTONES
1: Start at trailhead; 2: Outcrop viewpoint; 3: Knob Point; 1: Return to trailhead.

Steller's Jay

GO GREEN | The nonprofit Carson Valley Trails Association is a volunteer group dedicated to providing access to public lands through a network of local trails. You can learn more about their mission and their work in and around the Carson Valley at www.carsonvalleytrails.org.

OPTIONS | Strong hikers and mountain bikers could continue up the Clear Creek Trail to additional landmarks, or all the way to a connection with the Tahoe Rim Trail at Spooner Summit, a total of 14.5 miles. At 8 miles, there is a junction with the 2-mile Clear Creek Connector, which presently dead-ends at the boundary of state property but will hopefully have trailhead access at some point in the future. Arrangements for a shuttle offers the possibility of a one-way hike along the entire length of the Clear Creek Trail from Spooner Summit downhill to Jacks Valley.

Additional Trips

EZ TRAIL | 39°08.900'N, 119°46.224'W From a trailhead on South Curry Street behind the Nevada State Railroad Museum, a single-track trail (with short sections sharing a 4WD road) can be accessed that travels eastbound to the dirt road system connecting with the Kings Canyon Road.

CHAPTER THREE

THE MOUNTAINS

Mountains seemingly appear in nearly every corner of Eagle Valley. The most dominant range is the Carson, a subrange of the Sierra Nevada, its steep escarpment rising in dramatic fashion above the plain in the west. Across the valley to the east are the lower Pine Nut Mountains, a typical Great Basin range with tan-colored slopes. At the north end is the southern extent of the Virginia Range, where McClellan Peak is one of Carson City's most prominent landmarks. The only significant gaps in this ring of peaks occur where the Carson River has carved a path into and out of the valley. All twelve of the trips in this chapter are located in the Carson Range, where the USFS administers most of the land and motorized travel is limited, which creates a more favorable environment for two- and four-legged recreationists.

TRIP 29 | Ophir Creek Trail: Davis Creek Park to Tahoe Meadows

The Ophir Creek Trail offers a fascinating glimpse into the geology and botany of the Carson Range. However, that glimpse comes at a price, as the 8-mile trail climbs almost continuously from just above the floor of Washoe Valley to subalpine Tahoe Meadows, gaining almost 4,000 feet of elevation on the way. (Obviously, reversing the direction makes the trip much easier physically.) You will still be able to see the results of the devastating slide of 1983, when a piece of aptly named Slide Mountain slid into Lower Price Lake, sending a gooey mass of debris down Ophir Creek canyon and across Washoe Valley. You will also experience several different environments on the way, including Jeffrey pine forest, riparian zones along Ophir Creek, mixed montane forest above 6,500 feet, and lovely subalpine meadow. Short side trips to Rock and Price Lakes expand the variety even further.

LEVEL	Hike, advanced
LENGTH	8.1 miles, shuttle
TIME	3/4 day
ELEVATION	+3,875'/−350'
USERS	Hikers, trail runners, mountain bikers, equestrians
DOGS	On leash (first and last miles)
DIFFICULTY	Strenuous
SEASON	June to October
BEST TIME	Late June to early July
FACILITIES	Campground, horseshoe pits, lake, picnic areas, restrooms, volleyball area
MAPS	Humboldt-Toiyabe National Forest: *Mount Rose Wilderness*; USGS: *Mount Rose*
MANAGEMENT	Washoe County Parks and Open Space at 775-328-3600, www.washoecounty.us/parks; USFS Humboldt-Toiyabe National Forest-Carson Ranger District at 775-882-2766, www.fs.usda.gov/htnf
HIGHLIGHTS	Autumn color, canyon, forest, lakes, meadow, stream, wildflowers
LOWLIGHTS	Rough, steep, and indistinct sections of trail; poorly signed

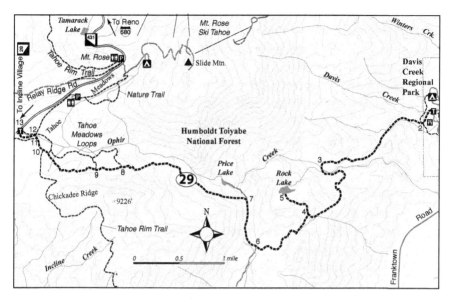

29. Ophir Creek Trail: Davis Creek Park to Tahoe Meadows

TIP | If you're not up to the nearly continuous eight-mile climb from Davis Creek Park to Tahoe Meadows, reversing the direction is straightforward and much less physically taxing.

KID TIP | Steep and poor tread makes this trail ill suited for younger children. The Nature and Discovery Trails inside Davis Creek Park (Trip 41) would be much better options.

TRAILHEAD START | 39°18.307′N, 119°50.039′W From Carson City, follow I-580 northbound toward Reno. Take Exit 50 and follow signs for Davis Creek Park, turning left from the off-ramp and immediately turning right into the park entrance. Follow the park road past the equestrian trailhead, park headquarters, and campground entrance to the signed trailhead on the right, 0.3 mile from the entrance.

END | For the shuttle option, follow I-580 to the Mt. Rose Highway Exit 56. From there, head southwest on State Route 431 toward North Lake Tahoe. After 15 miles you pass the large parking lot for the Mt. Rose trailhead on the right, near the high point of the highway (8911′), which is the highest road summit open all year in the Sierra Nevada. Continue another 1.1 miles to the far end of Tahoe Meadows and park on the shoulder as space allows. The trail begins on the east side of the highway (no facilities). 39°18.136′N, 119°55.095′W.

Equestrians below Slide Mountain on the Ophir Creek Trail

TRAIL | Head up the hillside through light Jeffrey pine forest and pass by an unmarked trail from below. Follow winding tread to a wood-plank bridge spanning lushly lined Davis Creek, and keep climbing to a signed junction [2] with the Discovery Trail, 0.2 mile from the trailhead. Continue straight ahead from the junction, passing another unmarked trail at 0.4 mile. Just beyond, the Ophir Creek Trail bends into the canyon of a tributary stream and climbs stiffly up this ravine. The steep climb abates briefly alongside a lush meadow, but the upward slog quickly resumes. Ignore an unmarked trail heading off to the left and veer to the right here, as the grade eases and briefly descends toward the edge of Ophir Creek canyon. Reach a viewpoint, where keen eyes can still detect evidence of the 1983 slide.

Resume the climb away from the vista point and proceed through a light Jeffrey pine forest with an understory of scattered shrubs. Follow the trail away from the canyon for a bit until you encounter a wide, rock-filled swath, left behind from the big slide. Leaving the edge of the forest, you cross Ophir Creek [3] at 1.6 miles, which should be a straightforward boulder hop unless the creek is swollen with snowmelt early in the season. The route of the trail is not obvious here amid the rock debris, but you should find the resumption of a defined single-track trail on the far side.

Away from Ophir Creek, the trail veers downstream for a bit and then drops around the nose of a forested ridge above the south side of the creek. Merge with the track of an old road and climb steeply up a long gully past point 5465. Head across a hillside above the canyon of a seasonal stream and come to a signed junction [4] with the 0.5-mile lateral to Rock Lake, 3.0 miles from the trailhead.

SIDE TRIP TO ROCK LAKE | To visit Rock Lake, follow a gently graded stretch of trail north-northwest through Jeffrey pine forest for about 0.2 mile, followed by a moderate descent across a manzanita-covered hillside to the floor of the basin containing the lake. Reach the boulder-strewn shoreline of the aptly named lake, [5] where a sea of talus encircles the lake and fills the basin. The only break in the rock occurs along the northwest shore, where a patch of grass provides a suitable campsite for backpackers. Lily pads cover the water's surface, which provides a fine sight in early season. Without an inlet, the lake level drops over the course of the summer and becomes less attractive, especially following winters of light snowfall. After visiting the lake, retrace your steps to the Ophir Creek Trail junction. **[4] END SIDE TRIP**

Back on the Ophir Creek Trail, you make a stiff climb through moderate forest cover to the top of a minor ridge, where the trees thin and the hillside is studded with boulders and interesting-looking rock outcrops. Gently graded tread heads across the ridge and down to a junction [6] with the dirt surface of Little Valley Road at 3.9 miles.

Turn right and follow the road north, climbing and then traversing across the hillside. Gaps in the forest permit views downslope of Rock Lake and eastward to Washoe Lake. A half mile from the road/trail junction, you encounter a junction [7] with a single-track trail on the left, which is the continuation of the Ophir Creek Trail.

SIDE TRIP TO PRICE LAKE | To visit Price Lake, continue ahead on the road a short way past a diversion ditch to a ford of Ophir Creek. This ford may be difficult in early season and will most likely be a wet crossing at other times except late in the summer when the outflow from the lake is low. Across the creek, continue on the road briefly to reach the east shore. **END SIDE TRIP**

From the Little Valley Road / Ophir Creek Trail junction, [7] the trail resumes its climbing ways, steeply ascending the hillside above Price Lake through mixed forest, where mountain hemlocks, western white pines, and white firs join the Jeffrey pines. Farther on, cross a pair of spring-fed, lushly lined rivulets and keep climbing into stands of more open forest alternating with small patches of verdant meadow. In early season, the meadows are peppered with an abundance of colorful wildflowers. As the ascent continues, the trail stays away from the creek and enters a dense lodgepole pine forest. Reach a marked junction [8] with the Tahoe Meadows Lower Loop, 6.2 miles from the trailhead.

Proceed ahead from the junction and follow the wide track of an old road through a mixed forest of Jeffrey pines, mountain hemlocks, western

Slide Mountain brought destruction in 1983

white pines, and white firs. After 0.3 mile, you come to a junction with the Middle Loop. [9]

The Ophir Creek Trail continues climbing on a generally westward course. After a bit, the ascent ends, giving way to a gentle descent through mostly lodgepole pine forest. Where the grade eases, you encounter the Ophir Creek Trail signboard and reach a Y junction [10] with the Tahoe Rim Trail angling southeast behind you.

On the shared route of the Tahoe Rim and Ophir Creek Trails, continue ahead, soon emerging from the trees to walk along the fringe of Tahoe Meadows. Reach the next junction, [11] with a path providing mountain bikers direct access to the Mt. Rose Highway. Follow the right-hand trail and wander around toward a bridge over Ophir Creek and a boardwalk just beyond. Just before the bridge is a junction, [12] where you turn left and proceed on a single-track trail toward the edge of the highway. Just before the road is a short bridge across Ophir Creek. From there, climb a set of stairs up to the end of the trip at the shoulder of the Mt. Rose Highway. [13]

PRICE LAKE Before the slide in the spring of 1983, there were two lakes tucked beneath the southeast slope of Slide Mountain, Upper and Lower Price Lakes. After oversaturation from melting snow, a massive flank of the mountain slid into Lower Price Lake, displacing the water and forming a semiliquid mass that roared down the canyon like a freight train, wiping out homes in Washoe Valley and spilling tons of debris across the freeway. When the dust settled, Lower Price Lake was gone, Upper Price Lake was reduced in size, and Ophir Creek canyon was considerably altered. Unfortunately, along with extensive property damage, the slide claimed one life.

MILESTONES

1: Start at Ophir Creek trailhead; **2:** Straight at Discovery Trail junction; **3:** Cross Ophir Creek; **4:** Rock Lake junction; **5:** Rock Lake; **4:** Return to Ophir Creek Trail; **6:** Right at Little Valley Road; **7:** Left at Ophir Creek Trail junction; **8:** Straight at Lower Loop junction; **9:** Straight at Middle Loop junction; **10:** Straight at Tahoe Rim Trail junction; **11:** Right at junction; **12:** Left at junction; **13:** End at Mt. Rose Highway.

GO GREEN | You can assist the Humboldt Toiyabe National Forest by volunteering for short-term or seasonal projects. For more information, visit the volunteer page at www.fs.usda.gov/main/r4/jobs/volunteer.

OPTIONS | Leaving a cooler filled with your favorite beverages in the car at Tahoe Meadows will be greatly appreciated after the long and stiff climb from Washoe Valley. As mentioned in the introduction, reversing the direction of this trip will require much less physical energy.

Ash Canyon Road to Snow Valley Peak

For those up to the task, the route of the Ash Canyon Road to the top of Snow Valley Peak offers a long and strenuous journey to outstanding views from the 9,214-foot summit.

LEVEL	Hike, advanced
LENGTH	13 miles, Out and back
TIME	Full day
ELEVATION	+3,800'/−300'
USERS	Hikers, trail runners, mountain bikers, equestrians
DOGS	OK
DIFICULTY	Strenuous
SEASON	Late June to November
BEST TIMES	Late June to early July, October
FACILITIES	None
MAP	USGS: *Carson City, Marlette Peak*
MANAGEMENT	USFS Humboldt-Toiyabe National Forest-Carson Ranger District at 775-882-2766, www.fs.usda.gov/htnf
HIGHLIGHTS	Autumn color, canyon, forest, stream, summit, views
LOWLIGHTS	Rough, steep, and poorly signed; road open to off-highway vehicles (OHV) below Lake Tahoe Nevada State Park boundary

TIP ı Get an early start to beat the heat, as the initial stretch of the route is steep and lacks shade. A weekday visit may minimize the OHV traffic.

KID TIP ı Not the best choice for small children, as the route is very strenuous and open to motorized vehicles. The shorter and easier trips in the Ash Canyon area (Trips 19–20) are much better suited for youngsters.

TRAILHEAD START ı 39°10.698'N, 119°49.405'W From North Carson Street, drive west on West Winnie Lane for 1.4 miles and turn right onto Ash Canyon Road. Head west on Ash Canyon Road for 0.5 mile to the end of the housing development, where the road bends and makes a winding ascent to the vicinity of a pair of water tanks. At the end of the pavement, continue ahead past the tanks a short distance to a small reservoir and then continue

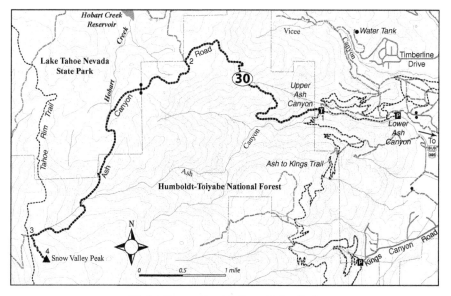

30. Ash Canyon Road to Snow Valley Peak

up the dirt road another mile to the parking area for the upper Ash Canyon trailhead.

TRAIL | From the upper Ash Canyon trailhead, you follow the continuation of the Ash Canyon Road out of the main canyon on a winding ascent to the top of a knoll at one mile, which offers a fine view of Eagle Valley backdropped by the Pine Nut Mountains.

Beyond the knoll, the road continues to snake up the east side of the Carson Range for a while until the grade eases. A 0.75-mile section of gradually rising tread leads to an unmarked junction [2] with a road heading toward Hobart Reservoir, 2.75 miles from the trailhead.

Veer to the left at the junction and resume the stiff climbing that eventually eases again on the way through a mixed forest of lodgepole, Jeffrey, and western white pines. Reach another knoll with good views of the valley below and of Carson City. Farther on, Snow Valley Peak momentarily pops into view. Walk around a closed steel gate at the east boundary of Lake Tahoe Nevada State Park and follow a gently graded section of road through dense forest, briefly following a stretch of a willow-lined tributary of Hobart Creek. From there, a mildly undulating climb leads upslope, with occasional, filtered views of Marlette and Herlan Peaks to the east and Mt. Rose and Slide Mountain to the north.

A more moderate climb heads up to a forested saddle. Drop down from the saddle and then follow an arcing route into the willow-lined Ash Canyon

View looking down Ash Canyon

Creek drainage. Travel upstream for a bit, cross the creek, and climb through stands of forest alternating with patches of meadow on the way to a junction [3] at the crest of the Carson Range.

Turn left at the junction and follow an old jeep track toward the top of Snow Valley Peak. Reach the summit [4] of the 9,214-foot peak after a 0.4-mile winding climb. The highlight of the excellent 360-degree vista is Lake Tahoe to the west, with Marlette Lake directly below. Pack along a map covering a large enough area to help you identify the numerous landmarks seen from the lofty aerie. When the time comes, retrace your steps to the parking area. [1]

MOUNTAIN BLUEBIRD (*Sialia currucoides*) The state bird of Nevada, the mountain bluebird is found in the higher elevations during summer. The males are beautifully colored, sky-blue birds and rather small at six inches long and weighing just an ounce, but they are a stunning sight perched in a whitebark pine tree or in flight. A member of the thrush family, they hunt insects, are monogamous, and nest in cavities.

MILESTONES
1: Start at Ash Creek Road parking area; 2: Turn left at junction with road to Hobart Reservoir; 3: Turn left at junction; 4: Snow Valley Peak; 1: Return to parking area.

GO GREEN | The Great Basin Group of the Toiyabe chapter of the Sierra Club is based in Reno. They are very involved in getting people outdoors, as well as participating in environmental matters. To learn more about their mission and activities, consult the website at www.sierraclub.org/toiyabe/great -basin/.

OPTIONS | Leaving a second vehicle at the Spooner Summit trailhead could create a shuttle trip that would shorten the trip by nearly 2 miles and offer the opportunity to see some different terrain from what you would see by simply backtracking to the Ash Canyon trailhead. From the summit of Snow Valley Peak, reverse the description in Trip 31 and follow the Tahoe Rim Trail southbound to the Spooner Summit trailhead at US 50.

Tahoe Rim Trail: Spooner Summit to Snow Valley Peak

Stunning views from the top of Snow Valley Peak highlight the trip to the summit. However, you must endure 5 miles of hiking through viewless forest before breaking out of the trees to your first sweeping views of Lake Tahoe and the surrounding terrain. A trio of vista points easily accessed from the Tahoe Rim Trail offers limited views within the first couple of miles, providing a modicum of inspiration for continuing all the way to Snow Valley Peak or good turnaround points for shorter hikes.

LEVEL	Hike, intermediate
LENGTH	12.4 miles, out and back
TIME	3/4 day
ELEVATION	+2,450'/–450'
USERS	Hikers, trail runners
DOGS	OK
DIFFICULTY	Moderately strenuous
SEASON	Mid-June through October
BEST TIME	Late June to mid-July
FACILITIES	Interpretive signs
MAPS	USGS: *Glenbrook, Marlette Lake* (trail not shown); Lake Tahoe Nevada State Park (LTNSP): *Marlette-Hobart Backcountry* (www.parks.nv.gov/forms/Spooner_backcountry _map.pdf)
MANAGEMENT	USFS Humboldt-Toiyabe National Forest-Carson Ranger District at 775-882-2766, www.fs.usda.gov/htnf
HIGHLIGHTS	Autumn color, forest, summit, views
LOWLIGHTS	Lack of water

TIP | Get an early start in order to secure a parking place on busy summer weekends.

KID TIP | This would be a rather long hike for small children—Spooner Lake would be a better option nearby.

TRAILHEAD | 39°06.266′N, 119°53.820′W Follow US 50 west from South Carson Street about 9 miles to the signed Tahoe Rim Trail (TRT) trailhead on

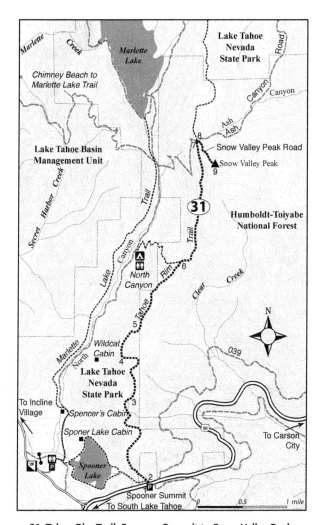

31. Tahoe Rim Trail: Spooner Summit to Snow Valley Peak

the right-hand shoulder, which is 0.75 mile east of the junction of Nevada State Route 28 (SR 28).

TRAIL | The well-signed trail begins a gentle climb away from the parking lot, soon passing a junction [2] on the left with a trail descending toward Spooner Lake in Lake Tahoe Nevada State Park below. Beyond the junction the grade increases to moderate through a forest of Jeffrey pines and red firs, with very brief glimpses of Spooner Lake through the dense timber. Continue the forested ascent, reaching a short side trail [3] leading to a viewpoint of Clear Creek canyon and serpentine US 50 at 1.3 miles.

Near the summit of Snow Valley Peak

Keep climbing away from the junction, as the trail bends around low hills and across minor ridges on the way to the next viewpoint lateral [4] at 1.9 miles, where another short path leads to the top of a boulder-studded mound offering views of Carson Valley to the east and summits above Desolation Wilderness to the southwest.

Another stretch through viewless forest brings you to the top of a ridge, 2.25 miles from the trailhead, where a longer lateral [5] heads toward a pile of boulders on a knoll offering your first view of the deep blue waters of Lake Tahoe. If you're looking for a short trip that's not too difficult, this vista offers a good turnaround point for a fine morning or afternoon hike.

Those bound for the summit of Snow Valley Peak should continue northbound on the TRT, which roughly follows the Carson Range crest on a steady climb through more forest cover for the next 1.75 miles. Beyond, the grade eases a bit on the way to a junction [6] with a trail on the left that drops 700 feet in 1.2 miles to connect with the North Canyon Road near the North Canyon Campground (one of only three spots backpackers can legally camp within Lake Tahoe Nevada State Park).

From the junction, a gently graded ascent finally leads out of the forest to open slopes across the east side of the Carson Range, offering good views of Carson Valley backdropped by the Pine Nut Mountains. The trail switchbacks to the west side of the ridge, where a superlative view unfolds of Lake Tahoe and the mountains along the Sierra crest. The views are interrupted by small groves of trees, but eventually you emerge onto completely open slopes of sagebrush, tobacco brush, and bitterbrush below the south ridge of Snow Valley Peak. For those not up to the full trip to the top, the beautiful views from this slope should be more than rewarding.

The TRT continues the rising ascent toward a saddle northwest of the summit, where you reach a four-way junction [7] with an old jeep road, 5.8 miles from the trailhead. The left-hand road descends stiffly to join the North Canyon Road south of Marlette Lake, the TRT continues ahead along the Carson Range crest, and the right-hand road soon leads down into Ash Canyon.

Turn right and briefly follow the road to an unmarked junction with an old road angling southeast on a 0.4-mile, winding ascent to the top of Snow Valley Peak. The 9,214-foot summit offers an expansive vista of the Tahoe Basin, although the topography is such that you may have to move about a bit to take advantage of the best viewpoints. Lake Tahoe is certainly the centerpiece of the 360-degree panorama, which also includes Carson Valley, Carson City, Eagle Valley, Washoe Lake and Valley, and the Truckee Meadows. A small-scale map of the area will be helpful in identifying the numerous geographical landmarks visible from this lofty aerie. When the time comes, retrace your steps to the trailhead. [1]

YELLOW-BELLIED MARMOT (*Marmota flaviventris*) The rock-filled slopes below Snow Valley Peak create a fine habitat for this member of the squirrel family. These four- to eleven-pound rodents dig their burrows underneath rocky slopes to avoid predators, which include coyotes and golden eagles in western Nevada. Marmots spend a great percentage of time in their burrows, hibernating during winter months and escaping the midday heat in summer. The best opportunities to observe them typically occur while they are sunning themselves in the morning or foraging in late afternoon. However, the chances of hearing their characteristic whistles of alarm are usually greater than actually seeing one of these chubby-looking rodents up close.

MILESTONES

1: Start at Spooner Summit trailhead (north); 2: Straight ahead at Spooner Lake junction; 3: First vista point lateral; 4: Second vista point lateral 5: Third vista point lateral; 6: Straight ahead at junction; 7: Turn right at four-way junction; 8: Turn right at road to top of Snow Valley Peak; 9: Summit of Snow Valley Peak; 1: Return to trailhead.

GO GREEN | Friends of Nevada Wilderness have been quite active within the Mt. Rose Wilderness and the Carson Range with such projects as eradicating

Yellow-Bellied Marmot

nonnative weeds and reseeding areas burned by forest fires. Check out their website at www.nevadawilderness.org.

OPTIONS | With a little extra effort, you could arrange a loop trip by descending from the four-way junction (**7**) west down the Ash Canyon Road to the North Canyon Road and then heading southbound to Spooner Lake. Follow the south part of the loop around Spooner Lake to a junction on the east side with the lateral climbing uphill to a junction with the TRT; then turn right to walk a very short distance to the Spooner Summit trailhead (**1**).

Tahoe Rim Trail: Spooner Summit to South Camp Peak

This section of the Tahoe Rim Trail offers hikers one of the grandest views of the Lake Tahoe Basin from the broad, mile-long plateau of South Camp Peak's summit. The effort involved in reaching the incredible vista is significant—a 5-mile hike gaining 1,875 feet—but will be quickly forgotten once the magnificent scenery unfolds.

LEVEL	Hike, intermediate
LENGTH	10.4 miles, out and back
TIME	3/4 day
ELEVATION	+1,875'/−225'
USERS	Hikers, trail runners, mountain bikers, equestrians
DOGS	OK
DIFFICULTY	Moderate
SEASON	Mid-June through October
BEST TIME	Late June to mid-July
FACILITIES	Picnic area, vault toilets
MAP	USGS: *Glenbrook* (trail not shown)
MANAGEMENT	USFS Humboldt-Toiyabe National Forest-Carson Ranger District at 775-882-2766, www.fs.usda.gov/htnf
HIGHLIGHTS	Autumn color, forest, summit, views
LOWLIGHTS	Lack of water

TIP I Be sure to pack plenty of water, as absolutely none is available en route to South Camp Peak.

KID TIP I This would be a rather long hike for small children—Spooner Lake would be a better option nearby.

TRAILHEAD I 39°06.229′N, 119°53.711′W Follow US 50 west from South Carson Street about 9 miles to the entrance into the signed Tahoe Rim Trailhead (south) on the left-hand shoulder, which is 0.75 mile east of the junction of SR 28. Park your vehicle in the parking lot as space allows.

TRAIL I This southbound stretch of the Tahoe Rim Trail follows a stiff climb via switchbacks up the hillside above US 50 through scattered Jeffrey pine and quaking aspen forest with a dense understory composed of chinquapin,

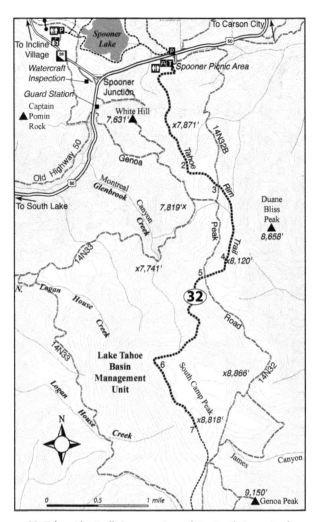

32. Tahoe Rim Trail: Spooner Summit to South Camp Peak

currant, manzanita, sagebrush, and tobacco brush. The ascent leads to the top of a ridge, where the grade eases to gently rising. Continue through selectively logged forest, with filtered views of Lake Tahoe to the west and Carson Valley to the east. Early-summer visitors will be treated to widely distributed wildflowers, such as lupine, mule ears, and paintbrush. Around the 1.5-mile mark, you reach the top of a rise and an unmarked junction [2] with a short side trail leading to a fine view.

Beyond the junction, the trail gently descends and then gently rises on the way to the crossing of dirt USFS Road 14N32B [3] at 2.5 miles from

Hikers on the Tahoe Rim Trail

the trailhead. Follow a gently graded rising traverse across a hillside below Duane Bliss Peak, cross an abandoned dirt road, and then gain the Carson Range crest once more. Moderate climbing along the crest leads to an unmarked junction near a rock hump, [4] where a short path leads up the hump to a pleasant view to the east of Carson Valley bordered by the Pine Nut Mountains. Back on the TRT, a gently graded descent heads away from the viewpoint into a forest of Jeffrey pines, red firs, and western white pines to a crossing of the well-traveled Genoa Peak Road (USFS Road 14N23), [5] 3 miles from the trailhead.

Climb moderately away from Genoa Peak Road into another section of selectively logged forest, where early-season visitors should be treated to a fair display of wildflowers. After quite a while, the trail switchbacks, bends around toward the southwest, and gains more elevation. The slightly higher altitude and aspect allows mountain hemlocks and lodgepole pines to join the mixed forest on the approach to the north edge of the broad summit plateau of South Camp Peak. Here you break out of the trees to a fine view of Lake Tahoe, improved by a short climb to the top of a rocky knoll, [6] where you'll enjoy perhaps one of the finest lake views on the TRT circuit. A small-scale map of the area will be helpful in identifying the numerous geographical landmarks visible from this fine perch.

The nearly flat terrain atop South Camp Peak stretches south before you for the next mile, with continuous views of the lake. Near the far edge of the plateau is the highest spot on the peak accessible by trail, where a handcrafted log bench [7] allows visitors a seat to enjoy the supreme view. When the time comes, retrace your steps to the trailhead. [1]

DUANE L. BLISS (1833–1907) While hiking along this section of the Tahoe Rim Trail, you may notice the forested slopes leading up to Duane Bliss Peak. Bliss left Massachusetts as a teenager to sail to South America. Following the lure of the gold rush, he sailed to Panama to make the crossing of the isthmus in hopes of obtaining passage to California. He contracted Chagres fever on the overland journey but recovered and eventually reached the Golden State. Migrating to Nevada, he mined silver on the Comstock and became a partner in a bank that was eventually purchased by the Bank of California. With his profits, he purchased timberland at Lake Tahoe and, along with Henry M. Yerington, founded the Carson & Tahoe Lumber and Fluming Company, which moved to Glenbrook in 1873. He also built a small railroad to carry lumber from the mill in Glenbrook to a flume at Spooner Summit. South Camp Peak got its name from one of the company's logging camps on the west slope. In twenty-eight years of operation, practically the entire forest within the Tahoe Basin was cut down to support the Comstock Lode. (Almost all the forest you see today is second growth.) Bliss foresaw the end of the logging boom and hence turned his attention to tourism, constructing a passenger rail line from Truckee to Lake Tahoe, the Glenbrook Hotel, and a luxury steamboat to carry sightseers across the lake. Having become one of Nevada's most successful businessmen, Bliss passed away two days before Christmas in 1907.

MILESTONES

1: Start at Spooner Summit trailhead (south); **2:** Viewpoint; **3:** Cross USFS Road 14N32B; **4:** Viewpoint; **5:** Cross USFS Road 14N32; **6:** Rocky knoll; **7:** Log bench; **1:** Return to trailhead.

GO GREEN | You can assist the Lake Tahoe Basin Management Unit of the USFS by volunteering for short-term or seasonal projects. For more information, visit the volunteer page at www.fs.usda.gov/main/ltbmu/workingtogether/volunteering.

OPTIONS | With shuttle arrangements you could organize a one-way, 12.2-mile trip between Spooner Summit and the Kingsbury North trailheads. Instead of returning the way you came to South Camp Peak, simply continue southbound on the TRT before leaving it at the junction with the lateral to the Kingsbury North trailhead 38°59.790′N, 119°53.799′W.

Spooner Lake

A gently graded, 1.6-mile path encircles Spooner Lake, providing hikers of all ages a fine opportunity to enjoy the picturesque surroundings. Interpretive displays with information on the natural and human history of the area and park benches scattered around the lakeshore enhance the experience. Amateur naturalists will appreciate the biodiversity found along the loop, including Jeffrey pine forest, quaking aspen groves, wildflower-filled meadows, and patches of sagebrush scrub. A wide range of wildlife may be seen as well, particularly a number of bird species, including hawks, warblers, thrushes, chickadees, and nuthatches. The area boasts many fine locations for enjoying a picnic lunch, and hot summer days will lure swimmers into the cool waters of the lake. The lake also offers to opportunity for catch-and-release fishing.

LEVEL	Stroll, novice
LENGTH	1.8 miles, loop
TIME	1 hour
ELEVATION	Negligible
USERS	Hikers, trail runners
DOGS	On leash
DIFFICULTY	Easy
SEASON	May through October
BEST TIME	June to early July
FACILITIES	Bike rentals, cabins, camping (walk-in), interpretive programs, picnic area, restrooms, store
MAPS	LTNSP: *Marlette-Hobart Backcountry* (www.parks.nv.gov /forms/Spooner_backcountry_map.pdf); USGS: *Glenbrook*
MANAGEMENT	Lake Tahoe Nevada State Park at 775-749-0494, www.parks .nv.gov
HIGHLIGHTS	Autumn color, fishing (catch and release), interpretive signs, lake, wildflowers, wildlife
LOWLIGHTS	None

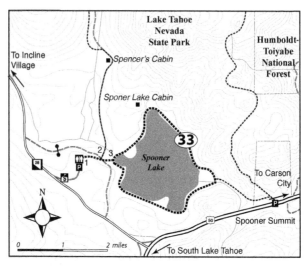

33. Spooner Lake

TIP | Visiting just after dawn or just before sundown increases your odds of seeing wildlife around the lake.

KID TIP | Spooner Lake is a wonderful place to take children of all ages. The lake offers a place for them to skip rocks or to drop a line for catch-and-release fishing between July 15 and September 30. Interpretive signs along the trail provide opportunities to teach them about the human and natural history of the area. Early summer offers wildflowers, while fall offers the turning leaves of quaking aspens. Enjoying a picnic lunch would be a fine complement to the hike.

TRAILHEAD | 39°06.430′N, 119°54.965′W Follow US 50 west from South Carson Street about 10 miles to the junction of SR 28. Turn right and head northwest for a mile to the entrance into Lake Tahoe Nevada State Park. After paying your fee ($8 for Nevada residents, $10 for nonresidents), follow signs to the parking area.

TRAIL | Follow signed directions from the parking area toward Spooner Lake and the start of the loop. **[2]** Turn left and proceed on a clockwise circuit around the lake, immediately crossing the dam. Improvements along the way include interpretive signs about the human and natural history of the area and periodically placed park benches for resting, enjoying the scenery, and watching the wildlife. You experience a nice variety of vegetation along the journey around the lake: large open areas carpeted with sagebrush, bitterbrush, and the yellow blooms of mule ears in early summer; pockets

Spooner Lake and Lake Tahoe

of willow; stands of Jeffrey pine and white fir away from the shoreline; and thick stands of quaking aspen near the inlet, where a sufficient amount of groundwater allows these trees to flourish. Working your way around to the southeast shore, you come to a junction [3] with a trail that climbs the slope to meet the Tahoe Rim Trail just a short way from the Spooner Summit trailhead.

Follow the right-hand path to continue the loop around the lake, soon crossing a wood bridge over Spooner Creek. Beyond the bridge, the route comes closer to the water's edge on the way through a wildflower-covered meadow. Oftentimes this is a great place to look for birdlife, including bald eagles, Canada geese, coots, ducks, herons, killdeer, and osprey. Continue around the lakeshore to the close of the loop [2] and then retrace your steps to the parking area. [1]

SPOONER LAKE The lake was originally a millpond built by the Carson & Tahoe Lumber and Fluming Company in the 1850s. After the logging boom, water from the lake was used for irrigation purposes when the dam was rebuilt in 1929. Along with Spooner Summit nearby, the lake was named for M. Spooner, owner of Spooners Station, a wood camp located not far from the present site of the lake.

1: Start at parking area; **2:** Left at loop junction; **3:** Veer right at junction with connector to TRT; **2:** Left at loop junction; **1:** Return to trailhead.

GO GREEN ❙ Nevada State Parks welcomes the assistance of volunteers who wish to support the parks with either their time or their pocketbooks. Check out the volunteer page on the state park website at www.park.snv.gov/about/volunteer-and-support.

OPTIONS ❙ Within the Spooner backcountry of Lake Tahoe Nevada State Park are two Scandinavian-style cabins available for rent. Spooner Lake Cabin, located on a knoll above the north shore of the lake, sleeps four while the more remote Wildcat Cabin, about three-quarters of a mile farther north, sleeps two. Both cabins are furnished with cook stoves, wood-burning stoves for heat, beds, and composting toilets. Contact Lake Tahoe Nevada State Park at spooner.rangeratgmail.com for more information.

Marlette Lake

Prior to 2005 all recreationists used to follow the North Canyon Road from Spooner Lake to Marlette Lake. Nowadays, the road is generally left to mountain bikers, who oftentimes connect with the legendary Flume Trail (see Trip 35) on a view-packed descent to Incline Village, as hikers (and equestrians) can follow the newer single track of the Marlette Lake Trail to the lake. All users still share the initial three-quarters of a mile on the road to where the trail splits off and travels through mixed forest to the high point of the journey just south of the lake, where a short descent leads to the shoreline.

LEVEL	Hike, intermediate
LENGTH	9 miles, out and back
TIME	1/2 day
ELEVATION	+1,225'/–400'
USERS	Hikers, trail runners, mountain bikers (road only), equestrians
DOGS	On leash
DIFFICULTY	Moderate
SEASON	Mid-June through October
BEST TIMES	Late June to mid-July, October
FACILITIES	Bike rentals, cabins, camping (walk-in), interpretive programs, picnic area, restrooms, store
MAPS	LTNSP: *Marlette-Hobart Backcountry* (www.parks.nv.gov /forms/Spooner_backcountry_map.pdf); USGS: *Glenbrook*
MANAGEMENT	Lake Tahoe Nevada State Park at 775-749-0494, www.parks .nv.gov
HIGHLIGHTS	Autumn color, fishing (catch and release), forest, interpretive signs, lake, wildflowers, wildlife
LOWLIGHTS	None

TIP ı Anglers must obey the fishing regulations at Marlette Lake, which include catch and release with artificial lures and single barbless hooks only between July 15 and September 30.

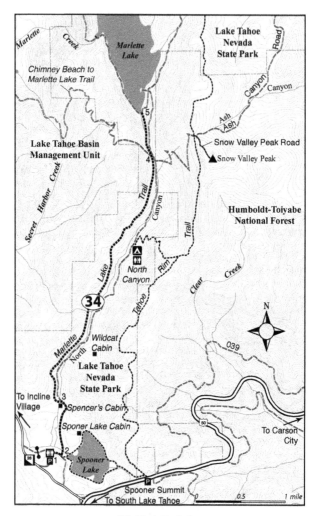

34. Marlette Lake

KID TIP | For older kids up to the task of hiking 9 miles, the out-and-back trip to Marlette Lake offers plenty of adventure. The lake is a fine spot for swimming following the mostly uphill hike, while the shoreline is well suited for dropping a line for catch-and-release fishing, and the lovely scenery provides an ideal backdrop for a picnic lunch. Kids can also poke around the old fish hatchery, which might be a good opportunity for them to learn about the two species of trout, rainbow and cutthroat, raised here, as well as the resident brook trout—visit the Nevada Department of Wildlife website and follow links at www.ndow.org for more information about the fish and Marlette Lake.

Marlette Lake

TRAILHEAD ⏐ 39°06.430′N, 119°54.965′W Follow US 50 west from South Carson Street about 10 miles to the junction of SR 28. Turn right and head northwest for a mile to the entrance into Lake Tahoe Nevada State Park. After paying your fee ($8 for Nevada residents, $10 for nonresidents), follow signs to the parking area.

TRAIL ⏐ Follow signed directions from the parking area for Marlette Lake toward the North Canyon Road. After 0.1 mile, you merge with the road and cross an open sagebrush flat before entering a mixed forest of lodgepole pines, white firs, and Jeffrey pines. Reach a junction [2] after about 0.25 mile with a side trail on the right to Spooner Lake Cabin, one of two Scandinavian-style cabins available for rent within the park. A short distance up the road is Spencer's Cabin on the left, an historical relic from the Comstock era. Continue up the road, shortly crossing the stream draining North Canyon and coming to the junction [3] between the road and the Marlette Lake Trail.

At this junction, mountain bikers are required to stay on the road, and hikers and equestrians are encouraged to use the trail. Veer to the left and follow a single-track trail on the west bank of the creek on steadily rising tread through moderate forest cover. About 2 miles from the parking lot, the trail crosses a diversion channel to Secret Harbor Creek and then continues the ascent for another 1.2 miles to a junction [4] with a short lateral to North Canyon Campground and the continuation of a steep, 1.2-mile connector to the Tahoe Rim Trail.

Remaining on the North Canyon Trail, you may notice the addition to the forest of quaking aspen trees, which put on a very showy display around mid-October. Reach a four-way junction [5] in a forested saddle dividing the North Canyon drainage from Marlette Lake's basin, 4 miles from the parking lot. The old road on the left heads toward Lake Tahoe on the route to the Chimney Beach trailhead, while the right-hand road shortly descends to the North Canyon Road and then zigzags up the east wall to a connection with the Tahoe Rim Trail near Snow Valley Peak.

Continue ahead at the junction, descending and crossing a couple of times a short stream that drains into Marlette Lake. After half a mile, you reach the southern tip of the lake [6] near a trout hatchery built in the late 1980s. Until 2006 fishing was not allowed in Marlette Lake, but nowadays catch-and-release fishing with artificial lures and barbless hooks is permitted between July 15 and September 30 for rainbow, brook, and cutthroat trout. A lone picnic table near the hatchery offers a fine spot for enjoying the view while eating a picnic lunch. Marlette Lake is part of the domestic water supply for Carson City, so camping is not allowed, but swimming and nonmotorized boating are acceptable. When your time at the lake is over, retrace your steps to the parking area. [1]

MARLETTE LAKE The earthen dam that holds back the waters of Marlette Lake was built in 1873 for the purposes of transporting water to Virginia City during the Comstock Lode era. Water from the dam was sent down a flume to Tunnel Creek Station, where the water went through a tunnel beneath the Carson Range and into flumes on the east side of the mountains to Lakeview. From there, an inverted siphon took the water up to Virginia City. Over the years, the dam was raised a number of times until reaching a height of forty-five feet in 1959. The state of Nevada purchased Marlette Lake and the neighboring land in 1963.

MILESTONES

1: Start at parking area; 2: Straight at Spooner Lake Cabin junction; 3: Veer right at Marlette Lake Trail junction; 4: Straight at North Canyon Campground junction; 5: Straight at Chimney Beach junction; 6: Marlette Lake; 1: Return to parking area.

GO GREEN | Nevada State Parks welcomes the assistance of volunteers who wish to support the parks with either their time or their pocketbooks. Check out the volunteer page on the state park website at www.park.snv.gov/about /volunteer-and-support.

OPTIONS | Options for further wanderings around Marlette Lake are numerous. Walking the North Canyon Road back to the parking area is certainly possible, but hikers should avoid doing so on busy weekends, as numerous mountain bikers will be using the road to access the notable Flume Trail, which begins near the dam on the west shore. At less busy times, hikers should still courteously hike single file along the edge of the road and be on constant lookout for bikers. From the south end of Marlette Lake, the road on the left heads toward the dam and the start of the Flume Trail (Trip 35). The road to the right travels around the southeast shore to access a little peninsula and then continues to a junction with the North Canyon Road; continuing northbound on the road leads to fine lake views and eventually a connection with the Tahoe Rim Trail.

Strong hikers who want to avoid backtracking to the parking area can create a loop trip by returning to the four-way junction, climbing up the connector trail to the Tahoe Rim Trail, following the TRT south to a junction a short distance before the Spooner Summit trailhead, and then descending to Spooner Lake and returning to the parking area.

35 | Flume Trail

0   500   1,000 feet

Tahoe's most famous and popular mountain bike trail follows in part the route of an old flume across the east slope of the Carson Range, offering unparalleled views and incomparable scenery. First, you have to get to the start of the Flume Trail by traveling to Marlette Lake's dam; hikers can follow the Marlette Lake Trail as described in the previous trip, while mountain bikers can ride up the North Canyon Road. After the four-mile romp on the Flume Trail, a stiff, three-mile descent leads to the ending trailhead near SR 28 at the south end of Incline Village. For those wanting to avoid using two vehicles, a shuttle service is available (see Options).

LEVEL	Hike, advanced
LENGTH	14 miles, shuttle
TIME	Full day
ELEVATION	+1,225'/−1,950'
USERS	Hikers, trail runners, mountain bikers (road only)
DOGS	On leash
DIFFICULTY	Strenuous
SEASON	Mid-June through October
BEST TIMES	Late June to mid-July, October
FACILITIES	Bike rentals, cabins, camping (walk-in), interpretive programs, picnic area, restrooms, store
MAPS	LTNSP: *Marlette-Hobart Backcountry* (www.parks.nv.gov /forms/Spooner_backcountry_map.pdf); USGS: *Glenbrook*
MANAGEMENT	Lake Tahoe Nevada State Park at 775-749-0494, www.parks .nv.gov
HIGHLIGHTS	Autumn color, fishing (catch and release), forest, interpretive signs, lake, wildflowers, wildlife
LOWLIGHTS	Exposure, lengthy, popular

TIP | While in-shape mountain bikers and trail runners will find the fourteen-mile distance within the normal range of their pursuits, the length will challenge some hikers. For those up to the task, get an early start, pack plenty of food and fluids, and carry gear for changing weather conditions.

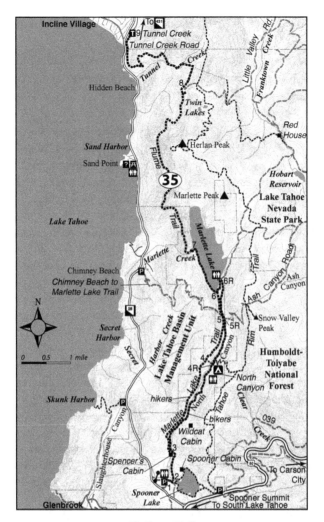

35. Flume Trail

KID TIP | The fourteen-mile journey might be considered long for most adults, let alone children. Spooner Lake would be a much better choice for small kids (see Trip 33) and Marlette Lake a better option for older children (see Trip 34).

TRAILHEAD START | 39°06.430′N, 119°54.965′W Follow US 50 west from South Carson Street about 10 miles to the junction of SR 28. Turn right and head northwest for a mile to the entrance into Lake Tahoe Nevada State Park.

After paying your fee ($8 for Nevada residents, $10 for nonresidents), follow signs to the parking area.

TRAILHEAD END | 39°14.097'N, 119°55.784'W The ending trailhead is about 10 miles from the entrance to Spooner Lake. On State Route 28, drive to Ponderosa Ranch Road near the south side of Incline Village and park in the lot across from the Tunnel Creek Café.

TRAIL | Follow signed directions from the parking area for Marlette Lake toward the North Canyon Road. After 0.1 mile, you merge with the road and cross an open sagebrush flat before entering a mixed forest of lodgepole pines, white firs, and Jeffrey pines. Reach a junction [2] after about 0.25 mile with a side trail on the right to Spooner Lake Cabin, one of two Scandinavian-style cabins available for rent within the park. A short distance farther up the road is Spencer's Cabin on the left, an historical relic leftover from the Comstock era. Continue up the road, shortly crossing the stream draining North Canyon and coming to the junction [3] between the road and the Marlette Lake Trail.

At this junction, mountain bikers are required to stay on the road, and hikers and equestrians are encouraged to use the trail. Veer to the left and follow a single-track trail on the west bank of the creek on steadily rising tread through moderate forest cover. About 2 miles from the parking lot, the trail crosses a diversion channel to Secret Harbor Creek and then continues the ascent for another 1.2 miles to a junction [4] with a short lateral to North Canyon Campground and the continuation of a steep, 1.2-mile connector to the Tahoe Rim Trail.

Remaining on the North Canyon Trail, you may notice the addition to the forest of quaking aspen trees, which put on a very showy display around mid-October. Reach a four-way junction [5] in a forested saddle dividing the North Canyon drainage from Marlette Lake's basin, 4 miles from the parking lot. The old road on the left heads toward Lake Tahoe on the route to the Chimney Beach trailhead, while the right-hand road shortly descends to the North Canyon Road and then zigzags up the east wall to a connection with the Tahoe Rim Trail near Snow Valley Peak.

Continue ahead at the junction, descending and crossing a couple of times a short stream that drains into Marlette Lake. After 0.5 mile, you reach the southern tip of the lake and a road junction [6] near a trout hatchery built in the late 1980s. Until 2006 fishing was not allowed in Marlette Lake, but nowadays catch-and-release fishing with artificial lures and barbless hooks is permitted between July 15 and September 30 for rainbow, brook, and cutthroat trout. A lone picnic table near the hatchery offers a fine spot for enjoying the view while eating a picnic lunch. Marlette Lake is part of the domestic water supply for Carson City, so camping is not allowed, but swimming and nonmotorized boating are acceptable.

At this junction, where mountain bikers rejoin the route, turn left and follow the level path around the south and west shores of Marlette Lake for about a mile to the dam. [4] After crossing the outlet and a brief section of technical trail, the most pleasurable part of the journey begins along the course of the old flume, where the forty-foot-per-mile grade offers periodically stunning views of Lake Tahoe. The path is narrow with some steep drop-offs in places, and you'll have to negotiate a rockslide, but the absolutely spectacular scenery will more than compensate for these minor hindrances. After 4 miles of the Flume Trail section, you intersect Tunnel Creek Road near a hairpin turn. [5]

Merge onto the sandy track of Tunnel Creek Road and head generally north to begin a much steeper descent toward Lake Tahoe's shore through light forest. After a 0.5 mile, you reach Tunnel Creek Station at the terminus of the old flume, where water was then sent east through a tunnel beneath the Carson Range to the flume system on the east side. Here the road bends sharply west and continues the stiff descent for 0.25 mile to a crossing of Tunnel Creek. The road follows the creek downstream for another 0.3 mile before veering to the northwest and then winding around to the west. Remain on the obviously better traveled Tunnel Creek Road at various intersections on a zigzagging descent until the road bends sharply

Max Jones negotiating a turn

north to parallel SR 28 about 100 feet below. Eventually you emerge back into civilization near the Tunnel Creek Café at the end of your journey. [1]

MAX JONES A decorated professional mountain biker, Max Jones and his wife, Patti McMullen, moved to Incline Village in 1982. Shortly thereafter, he became aware of the existence of an old flume built in the late 1800s to divert water from Marlette Lake to a tunnel, part of an elaborately engineered system that eventually delivered water all the way to Virginia City. On his first visit, he found the trail overgrown with dense vegetation and sections completely buried by rockslides. He spent subsequent trips clearing the trail of brush and repairing the damaged areas, mostly by himself and mostly just with simple hand tools. Eventually the Flume Trail was completely repaired and became one of the ten best mountain biking trails in the world according to numerous publications. In addition to the trail restoration, Jones and McMullen organized an annual ride on the Flume Trail for many years. Nowadays, the couple operates the Tunnel Creek Café and Flume Trail Mountain Bikes near the route's terminus.

MILESTONES
1: Start at Spooner Lake trailhead; **2:** Left at North Canyon Road junction; **3:** Left at Marlette Lake junction; **4:** Straight at Chimney Beach junction; **5:** Left at Marlette Lake junction; **6:** Cross Marlette Lake outlet; **7:** Merge with Tunnel Creek Road; **8:** End at Tunnel Creek trailhead.

GO GREEN | Established in 2010, the Tahoe Fund is a nonprofit organization dedicated to providing private funding for environmentally oriented projects within the Lake Tahoe Basin that focus on recreation, conservation, and education. Their signature project is a recently constructed section of bike trail from Incline Village to Sand Harbor. To learn more about their work, visit the website at www.tahoefund.org.

OPTIONS | The Tunnel Creek Café (tunnelcreekcafe.com) near the exit point is a fine place to start your day or regroup after the long haul from Spooner Lake. The café offers tasty breakfast and lunch fare, ice-cold beers, fruit smoothies, coffees, and teas. Flume Trail Mountain Bikes offers bike rentals and convenient shuttle service between the Tunnel Creek Café and Spooner Lake (www.flumetrailtahoe.com).

Chimney Beach

As with just about any public beach around Lake Tahoe, Chimney Beach is a popular destination for locals and visitors alike. The beauty of the basin and the clarity of the water don't need to be sold to beach lovers at Tahoe. The minimal amount of walking necessary to reach Chimney Beach is at least a deterrent to some of the less fit. The bottom line is don't expect to be alone here. The best advice is to visit on weekdays if possible and to get any early start to secure a parking spot.

LEVEL	Walk, novice
LENGTH	2.2 miles, loop
TIME	1 hour
ELEVATION	+150'/−350'
USERS	Hikers
DOGS	OK
DIFFICULTY	Strenuous
SEASON	April through November
BEST TIMES	Late June to mid-September
FACILITIES	Trash cans, vault toilets
MAPS	USGS: *Marlette Lake*
MANAGEMENT	Lake Tahoe Basin Management Unit at 530-882-2600, www .fs.usda.gov/ltbmu
HIGHLIGHTS	Beach, lake, scenery
LOWLIGHTS	Limited parking, section of route along highway, popular

TIP ǀ Get an early start to increase the odds of getting a parking space.

KID TIP ǀ Most kids love the beach, so you shouldn't have much trouble keeping the young ones entertained. Make sure you plaster on the sunscreen and have plenty of fluids available. *Note: some of the more remote stretches of beach beyond the south end of the trail may have nude sunbathers.*

TRAILHEAD ǀ 39°10.054′N, 119°55.599′W Follow US 50 west from South Carson Street about 10 miles to the junction of SR 28. Turn right and head northwest on SR 28 for 5.4 miles to the entrance into a signed USFS parking

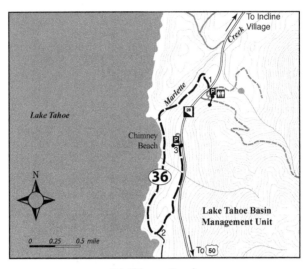

36. Chimney Beach

Lake Tahoe from Chimney Beach

lot on the east shoulder. Parking is limited, especially on summer weekends, so arrive early to secure a space.

TRAIL | From the parking lot, carefully cross SR 28 to the west shoulder and then follow gently descending single-track tread through a scattered forest of Jeffrey pines and white firs. Underneath the conifers, granite boulders

Black Bear

and a host of shrubs—including bitterbrush, chinquapin, manzanita, and tobacco brush—dot the slope. As you descend, incense cedars join the forest, as well as some deciduous varieties of trees. Follow a set of wood stairs down to a crossing of Marlette Creek on a wooden bridge.

On the far side of the bridge, the trail heads briefly downstream toward the shoreline of Lake Tahoe, where several social trails offer access to Chimney Beach. The remains of an old chimney lend the name to the sandy beach. Staying on the main trail, head south above the shoreline, immediately cross back over Marlette Creek, and proceed through scattered forest and groundcover, enjoying fine views of the lake and the mountains rising above the west side. Reach a Y junction [2] at 0.6 mile.

At the junction, the path ahead continues another 0.6 mile to more secluded sections of beach, where posted signs warn about the possibility of nude sunbathers. To return to the start of the trail, turn left and climb steeply uphill to the Secret Harbor parking lot. [3] Without a second vehicle or shuttle arrangements, you must walk back along the highway to the Chimney Beach parking lot. [1]

BLACK BEAR (*Ursus americanus*) The only species of bear found in Nevada, black bears are typically confined to the hills of the eastern Sierra as part of the Sierra Nevada population, which is estimated to include 10,000 to 15,000 individuals. Despite the name, these omnivores can also be shades of blonde, brown, or cinnamon. Some males can reach up to 600 pounds, but the average size is between 300 and 350 pounds. These fascinating mammals have rather poor eyesight, but their hearing is good, and they have an excellent sense of smell. Black bears are very fast runners, attaining speeds up to fifteen miles per hour. They are also good tree climbers.

MILESTONES

1: Start at Chimney Beach parking lot; **2:** Left at Y junction; **3:** Secret Harbor parking lot; **1:** Return to Chimney Beach parking lot.

GO GREEN ǀ Established in 2010, the Tahoe Fund is a nonprofit organization dedicated to providing private funding for environmentally oriented projects within the Lake Tahoe Basin that focus on recreation, conservation, and education. Their signature project is a recently constructed section of bike trail from Incline Village to Sand Harbor. To learn more about their work, visit the website at www.tahoefund.org.

OPTIONS ǀ Although there are no immediate plans, the goal is to have an accessible bike trail extending all the way around Lake Tahoe. When the recently constructed section from Incline Village to Sand Harbor is extended, access between the Chimney Beach and Secret Harbor parking lots should be greatly improved.

Chimney Beach to Marlette Lake

The Chimney Beach to Marlette Lake Trail is certainly considered the back way to Marlette Lake. Although longer, the standard route on the Marlette Lake Trail from Spooner Lake (Trip 34) gains 275 feet less over the course of an extra 1.5 miles at a much more pleasant grade. However, for those who prefer the road less traveled, this route shouldn't disappoint—perhaps without seeing any fellow hikers until reaching the lake. Although Marlette Lake is the main attraction, the Chimney Beach Trail draws near to a lushly lined tributary of Marlette Creek on the way up the hillside.

LEVEL	Hike, advanced
LENGTH	6 miles, out and back
TIME	Half day
ELEVATION	+1,500′/−175′
USERS	Hikers, trail runners, mountain bikers, equestrians
DOGS	OK
DIFFICULTY	Strenuous
SEASON	Mid-June through October
BEST TIMES	Late June to mid-July, October
FACILITIES	Trash cans, vault toilets
MAPS	LTNSP: *Marlette-Hobart Backcountry* (www.parks.nv.gov /forms/Spooner_backcountry_map.pdf); USGS: *Marlette Lake*
MANAGEMENT	Lake Tahoe Basin Management Unit at 530-882-2600, www .fs.usda.gov/ltbmu; Lake Tahoe Nevada State Park at 775-749-0494, www.parks.nv.gov
HIGHLIGHTS	Autumn color, fishing (catch and release), forest, interpretive signs, lake, stream, views, wildflowers, wildlife
LOWLIGHTS	Poorly maintained trail, steep

TIP I Get an early start to increase the odds of getting a parking space and to avoid making the steep climb during the hot part of the day.

KID TIP I Although relatively short, the steep and sometimes rough nature of the trail should discourage most parents from taking young children on

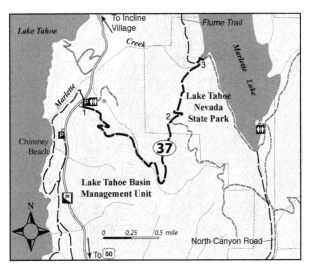

37. Chimney Beach to Marlette Lake

this hike. Spooner Lake would be a much better choice for small kids (see Trip 33) and Marlette Lake a better option for older children (see Trip 34).

TRAILHEAD | 39°10.054′N, 119°55.599′W Follow US 50 west from South Carson Street about 10 miles to the junction of SR 28. Turn right and head northwest on SR 28 for 5.4 miles to the entrance into a signed USFS parking lot on the east shoulder. Parking is limited, especially on summer weekends, so arrive early to secure a space.

TRAIL | Find the start of the Chimney Beach to North Canyon Trail on the south side of the parking lot beyond a closed steel gate at the start of a dirt road. The trip immediately starts climbing, soon doubling back where the track narrows on the way through a light, mixed forest of Jeffrey pines, western white pines, and white firs. Lake Tahoe can be seen through gaps in the trees, and the views improve with the gain in elevation. At 0.75 mile the grade eases for a bit on an arcing traverse around the hillside toward a lushly lined tributary of Marlette Creek, where alders, ferns, and thimbleberries thrive in the damp soils. The occasionally switchbacking trail climbs alongside the creek for a while and then crosses over to the north side on a short wood bridge. An ascending traverse leads across a slope of scattered Jeffrey pines, which allow a healthy understory of bitterbrush, manzanita, and tobacco brush to flourish. The climb steepens on the way to the top of a minor ridge and an indistinct junction, [2] 2.25 miles from the parking area. The right-hand trail heading generally southeast is the continuation of the Chimney Beach to North Canyon Trail.

View from the trail to North Canyon

Veer onto the left-hand trail, which does not appear on the LTNSP map, heading north-northeast from the top of the ridge on a short, gentle descent into a lush environment filled with aspens, grasses, small plants, and wildflowers. The dense foliage in this area can obscure the path in spots. Leaving this luxuriant glade behind, the trail starts climbing again across open slopes of bitterbrush, chinquapin, currant, pinemat manzanita, and tobacco brush. As the grade increases, Lake Tahoe and some of the peaks in Desolation Wilderness spring into view through gaps in the trees, and for the first time Marlette Lake makes an appearance. Eventually, you gratefully reach the apex of the climb.

After a short traverse from the high point, follow a steep, serpentine descent toward the slit of Marlette Creek's V-shaped canyon. On reaching the stream, you cross over and intersect the renowned Flume Trail [3] just below Marlette Lake's dam. Head upstream a short distance, and then walk across the top of the dam to the shoreline of the azure-blue lake. [4] After your explorations are complete, retrace your steps to the parking area. [1]

WESTERN WHITE PINE (*Pinus monticola*) One of the signature conifers in the mixed forest common in the Lake Tahoe Basin, the western white pine is found in only three ranges within Nevada beside the Carson Range, all in the far northwest part of the state. They grow in areas with plenty of light, not in dense stands. This majestic tree has blue-green

needles in bunches of five, with long (five- to ten-inch), slightly arcing cones. Bark on mature specimens is grayish brown, with distinctive
small square plates bordered by fine fissures.

MILESTONES

1: Start at Chimney Beach parking area; **2:** Veer left at junction; **3:** Turn
right at Flume Trail junction; **4:** Marlette Lake; **1:** Return to parking area.

GO GREEN | Established in 2010, the Tahoe Fund is a nonprofit organization
dedicated to providing private funding for environmentally oriented projects within the Lake Tahoe Basin that focus on recreation, conservation, and
education. Their signature project is a recently constructed section of bike
trail from Incline Village to Sand Harbor. To learn more about their work,
visit the website at www.tahoefund.org.

OPTIONS | Shuttle arrangements would allow you to create a point-to-point
trip by heading south from Marlette Lake on the Marlette Lake Trail to the
Spooner Lake trailhead.

TRIP
38 | Skunk Harbor

Skunk Harbor doesn't stink, as the crescent-shaped bay on the east shore of Lake Tahoe possesses lovely scenery, a sandy beach, and a bit of history in the old Newhall Mansion. To reach this little slice of Tahoe heaven requires either a boat or the willingness to hike down to the beach and back again. The 3.2-mile, round-trip journey is long enough to dissuade some people from accessing one of the lake's most stunning beaches, but this spot still receives plenty of adoration. The area is much quieter during the shoulder seasons, when sunbathers and swimmers are less interested in exposing themselves to the cooler temperatures.

LEVEL	Hike, intermediate
LENGTH	3.2 miles, out and back
TIME	2 hours
ELEVATION	+150'/−775'
USERS	Hikers, trail runners, mountain bikers
DOGS	OK
DIFFICULTY	Moderate
SEASON	Late May to mid-October
BEST TIME	Mid-June through September
FACILITIES	None
MAP	USGS: *Marlette Lake*
MANAGEMENT	Lake Tahoe Basin Management Unit at 530-882-2600, www.fs.usda.gov/ltbmu
HIGHLIGHTS	Beach, forest, history, lake, scenery
LOWLIGHTS	Limited parking, popular

TIP | As parking is severely limited, plan on arriving early to snag one of the spaces close to the start of the trail.

KID TIP | Most kids love the beach, so you shouldn't have much trouble keeping the young ones entertained. Make sure you plaster on the sunscreen and have plenty of fluids available. Make sure any young children possess the stamina for the all-uphill hike back to the car.

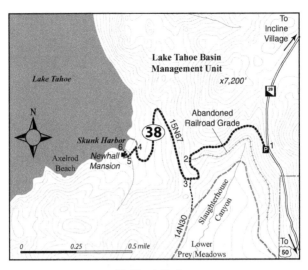

38. Skunk Harbor

TRAILHEAD ǀ 39°07.707′N, 119°55.871′W The trail begins near a closed steel gate just off SR 28 on the west shoulder, 2.4 miles north of the US 50 junction. Very limited parking may be available just north of the gate.

TRAIL ǀ Walk past the closed gate, and follow the course of an old road that at one time provided access to the Newhall Mansion on Tahoe's east shore. The road soon transitions from pavement to dirt, as you descend through a mixed forest of Jeffrey pines and white firs above an understory of shrubs, including buckwheat, chinquapin, manzanita, rabbitbrush, sagebrush, and tobacco brush. Early summer has added color from a sprinkling of purple lupines and yellow mule ears blossoms. Follow the road on a curve to the west around the head of Slaughterhouse Canyon above where the old railroad grade wraps around the steep slope below. About a half mile from the highway, you reach a junction **[2]** with the old railroad bed.

Continue ahead from the junction on road, which now adopts a steeper descent toward the south. After a quarter mile, the trail bends to the west again and reaches a small flat and an obscure junction **[3]** with a route on the left to Slaughterhouse Canyon (Trip 39).

Away from the junction, the road curves around and makes a long descending traverse across the forested hillside to the north-northwest. After a switchback, you travel south for a bit and then circle around to a three-way junction, **[4]** 1.5 miles from the trailhead, near the shore of the lake, where incense cedars join the forest and the understory becomes lusher. At the junction, the right-hand road follows the arc of Skunk Harbor's sandy beach to the north.

Kayakers on Lake Tahoe near Skunk Harbor

Turn left at the junction and walk a short distance on the road, crossing a short wood bridge over a pretty rivulet to a junction [5] where a single-track trail heads downstream toward the lake. Almost immediately the roof and walls of the old Newhall Mansion come into view, with a rock patio and outdoor fireplace nearby. Granite steps lead down to the old building. A short walk from there leads to the picturesque harbor with a sandy beach dotted with smooth granite boulders. [6] At the end of your visit, retrace your steps to the trailhead. [1]

STRIPED SKUNK (*Mephistis mephistis*) You're more apt to smell the presence of these nocturnal animals, members of the weasel family, than see one around Lake Tahoe. Their Latin name suitably comes from the word for bad odor. Although not aggressive, these cat-sized animals defend themselves quite effectively by spraying their musk on potential predators. The spray can travel up to twenty feet. The only consistent predator that is not totally deterred by the obnoxious spray is the great horned owl, which apparently must not have a highly developed sense of smell. The origin of the naming of Skunk Harbor is unclear, perhaps so named to deter visitors?

MILESTONES

1: Start at trailhead; **2:** Straight at railroad junction; **3:** Straight at junction; **4:** Left at junction; **5:** Right at single-track junction; **6:** Skunk Harbor; **1:** Return to trailhead.

GO GREEN I Under the familiar banner of "Keep Tahoe Blue," the League to Save Lake Tahoe has been assisting in protecting the quality of life at Lake Tahoe since 1957. You can learn more about their legacy and mission at www.keeptahoeblue.org.

OPTIONS I Other than the trip down Slaughterhouse Canyon described in Trip 39, there's pretty much nowhere else to go without some significant scrambling capabilities.

39 | Slaughterhouse Canyon

Most people who start out from the trailhead along SR 28 are bound for the beautiful shoreline of Lake Tahoe at Skunk Harbor. The present trip veers away for a more reclusive journey along part of the old course of a small railroad built in the 1800s to carry lumber from a mill in Glenbrook to a flume at Spooner Summit. The journey down Slaughterhouse Canyon is a pleasant walk past meadows and through shady forest to the end of USFS land at the boundary of the community of Glenbrook.

LEVEL	Hike, intermediate
LENGTH	5 miles, out and back
TIME	2 to 3 hours
ELEVATION	+0'/−550'
USERS	Hikers, trail runners, mountain bikers
DOGS	OK
DIFFICULTY	Moderate
SEASON	Late May to mid-October
BEST TIME	Mid-June through September
FACILITIES	None
MAP	USGS: *Marlette Lake*
MANAGEMENT	Lake Tahoe Basin Management Unit at 530-882-2600, www.fs.usda.gov/ltbmu
HIGHLIGHTS	Autumn color, forest, history, stream, wildflowers, wildlife
LOWLIGHTS	Limited parking

TIP ⏐ As parking is severely limited, plan on arriving early to snag one of the spaces close to the start of the trail.

KID TIP ⏐ After your return to Carson City following the hike to Slaughterhouse Canyon, you could opt for a visit to the Nevada State Railroad Museum, open Thursday to Monday from 9:00 A.M. to 4:00 P.M.; children under seventeen are admitted free. Check out the website for more information at www.nvculture.org/nevadastaterailroadmuseumcarsoncity/.

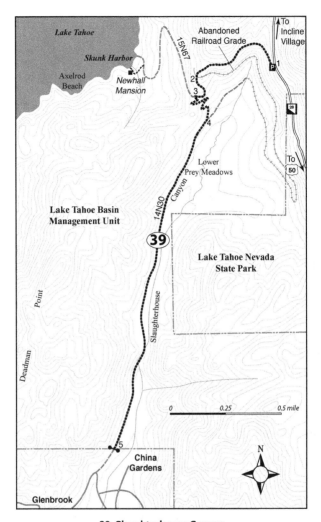

39. Slaughterhouse Canyon

TRAILHEAD | 39°07.707′N, 119°55.871′W The trail begins near a closed steel gate just off SR 28 on the west shoulder, 2.4 miles north of the US 50 junction. Very limited parking may be available just north of the gate.

TRAIL | Walk past the closed gate, and follow the course of an old road that at one time provided access to the Newhall Mansion on Tahoe's east shore. The road soon transitions from pavement to dirt, as you descend through a mixed forest of Jeffrey pines and white firs above an understory of shrubs, including buckwheat, chinquapin, manzanita, rabbitbrush, sagebrush, and tobacco brush. Early summer has the added color of a sprinkling of purple lupines and yellow mule ears blossoms. Follow the road on a curve to the west around the head of Slaughterhouse Canyon above where the old railroad grade wraps around the steep slope below. About a half mile from the highway, you reach a junction [2] with the old railroad bed.

Continue ahead from the junction on the road, which now adopts a steeper descent toward the south. After 0.25 mile, the trail bends to the west again and reaches a small flat and an obscure junction [3] with the route to Slaughterhouse Canyon on the left, 0.75 mile from the trailhead.

Turn left (south) at the flat, and locate a faint stretch of single-track tread winding downslope through Jeffrey pine forest. At the bottom of the slope, you reach a junction with the old railroad bed again. [4] Despite the faint noise of traffic from SR 28 and the presence of a power line paralleling the road, the gently graded journey down Slaughterhouse Canyon is quite pleasant, passing to the right of lovely, grass-covered Prey Meadows. Early-season visitors should be delighted by the wildflower display here, while autumn brings plenty of fall color from quaking aspens farther downstream. Farther on at Devils Gate, the canyon narrows, and the stream disappears in a small boulder field for a short stretch before the gorge widens out again and the creek reappears. Proceed through a shady forest of Jeffrey pines and white firs along the fringe of meadow-like vegetation near the water. Eventually you approach a steel gate [5] at the border of Glenbrook and the end of your journey. From there, retrace your steps to the trailhead. [1]

RAILROAD As part of the Carson & Tahoe Lumber and Fluming Company, Duane L. Bliss built a small railroad to carry lumber from a mill in Glenbrook to a flume at Spooner Summit. The grade that you walk on for a good portion of this trip follows that old railroad bed.

MILESTONES
1: Start at trailhead; 2: Straight at railroad grade; 3: Turn left at flat; 4: Veer right at railroad junction; 5: Glenbrook border; 1: Return to trailhead.

GO GREEN ⏐ You can assist the Humboldt Toiyabe National Forest by volunteering for short-term or seasonal projects. For more information, visit the volunteer page at www.fs.usda.gov/main/r4/jobs/volunteer.

OPTIONS ⏐ Other than the possibility of incorporating the journey down Slaughterhouse Canyon with the route to Chimney Beach, private property and the topography limit options for extending your trip.

Lam Watah Trail to Nevada Beach

While much of this end of Lake Tahoe is reserved for those with plenty of dough, the little slice of USFS land through which passes the Lam Watah Trail is available to the masses. Saved from the ignominy of housing hotel casinos, the area boasts an attractive pond lined with willows, a gurgling stream, stands of aspen and Jeffrey pine forest, flower-dotted meadows, and a very attractive strip of sandy beach along Lake Tahoe. During the height of summer, the beach is often crowded, but far fewer souls hike the short trail.

LEVEL	Walk, novice
LENGTH	2.2 miles, out and back
TIME	1 hour
ELEVATION	Negligible
USERS	Hikers, trail runners
DOGS	Not allowed on beach, OK on leash on trail
DIFFICULTY	Easy
SEASON	Late spring to early fall
BEST TIME	July to September
FACILTIES	Campground, picnic tables, restrooms, running water
MAP	USGS: *South Lake Tahoe*
MANAGEMENT	Lake Tahoe Basin Management Unit at 530-543-2600, www .fs.usda.gov/ltbmu
HIGHLIGHTS	Beach, fishing, scenery, swimming
LOWLIGHTS	Popular

TIP | While finding parking near the beach is usually a challenge in summer, locating a space at the trailhead should be much easier. However, the beach is generally crowded by midmorning and remains so until late in the day. Therefore, a hike early in the day or just before sundown may help to minimize exposure to the crowds.

KID TIP | Most children love the beach, so keeping the little ones engaged should be an easy task. Bring plenty of liquids, food, and sunscreen if you plan on spending the day.

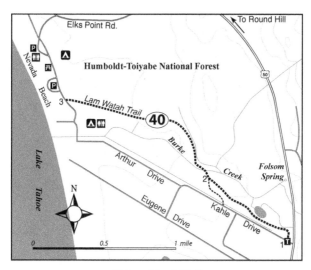

40. Lam Watah Trail

A willow-lined pond creates a beautiful scene on the Lam Watah Trail

TRAILHEAD ┃ The trailhead is located just off US 50, along Kahle Drive, which is 0.2 mile north of the Kingsbury Grade (SR 207) junction. Turn northwest onto Kahle, and park along the shoulder of the road as space allows.

TRAIL ┃ From the edge of Kahle Drive, cross the lush grasslands and foliage of a verdant meadow to the first interpretive sign, and soon pass by

Lam Watah Trail

a willow-lined pond and a copse of aspens. Walking by more interpretive signs, you meet a side [2] trail coming in from the left and then bend toward a log-plank bridge spanning Burke Creek. Continue past the bridge, and soon head into a pocket of light Jeffrey pine forest. Beyond the trees, you walk across a ribbon of meadow on an old jeep road, from where a number of use trails head into the forest to the north. After additional small sections of forest and meadow, you reach the Nevada Beach campground access road. A short distance to the west is the sandy beach and crystal-clear waters of Lake Tahoe. [3] When your time at the lake is over, retrace your steps to the trailhead. [1]

PRESERVING THE LAM WATAH TRAIL The property through which the Lam Watah Trail travels was once slated for the development of hotel casinos similar to those that dominate the skyline of Stateline. Fortunately, the Nature Conservancy purchased the land and subsequently donated it to the USFS. Left in a natural state, the area brings much enjoyment to visitors and residents alike. Lam Watah is a Washoe tribe term meaning "permanent mortar by the stream." Native Americans had a long history of camping in this area before the arrival of Europeans.

1: Start at trailhead; **2:** Straight at junction; **3:** Nevada Beach; **1:** Return to trailhead.

GO GREEN | The Nature Conservancy has not only been active in protecting lands around Lake Tahoe but also throughout the state of Nevada. To learn more about their work, volunteer for projects, or make a donation, check out the website at www.nature.org and follow the Our Work and Where We Work links to Nevada.

OPTIONS | Additional hikes in the vicinity are limited. If you prefer dining out to enjoying a picnic by the lake, there are numerous restaurants in the immediate area. On the way back to Carson City, Zephyr Cove Restaurant at the historic Zephyr Cove Resort has been serving breakfast, lunch, and dinner in a rustic and casual atmosphere since the early 1900s. Their homemade milkshakes and root beer floats are legendary.

CHAPTER FOUR

WASHOE VALLEY AND VIRGINIA CITY

North of Carson City lies a beautiful valley bordered by the hills of the Virginia Range to the east and the peaks of the Carson Range on the west. Tucked into a section of forest on the west side of the basin is Davis Creek Regional Park, where a pair of short and easy trails beckons recreationists. Within the boundaries of Washoe Lake State Park are a pair of lakes, Little Washoe and the much larger but shallower Washoe. Numerous hiking trails are available near the water's edge and in the hills above. To the east of the park, the Jumbo Grade trailhead provides multi-use access into the Virginia Range. Trips 48 and 49 follow routes beginning on the southwest side of the valley into the forest of the Carson Range on the way to Hobart Creek Reservoir. The last entry in this chapter is a challenging climb to Mt. Davidson perched directly above Virginia City. Plans in the greater area include a new trail connecting Carson City to Virginia City.

Davis Creek Park is tucked into the foothills near the east base of the Carson Range, complete with a campground, picnic area, and recreational facilities. The park also contains 2.5-acre Davis Pond, a fine spot for swimming or fishing when full. Within the park is a trio of hiking trails, including the Ophir Creek Trail (see Trip 29), which starts in the park before entering USFS land. Fully contained within the park boundaries are two loops, the 1.9-mile Discovery Trail and the 0.7-mile Nature Trail. The Discovery Trail follows a large loop through the park's distinct environments, Jeffrey pine forest on the hillsides, sagebrush scrub on the flats, riparian areas along the creeks, and the wetlands around the pond. The Nature Trail provides a shorter visit to all of those areas, with the added bonus of a brochure keyed to ten posts along the way.

41A ▪ Nature Trail

LEVEL	Stroll, novice
LENGTH	0.7 mile, loop
TIME	1/2 hour
ELEVATION	Negligible
USERS	Hikers, mountain bikers
DOGS	On leash
DIFFICULTY	Easy
SEASON	All year
BEST TIME	May through June
FACILITIES	Campground, fishing, horseshoe pits, picnic areas, restrooms, volleyball area
MAP	Washoe County Parks and Open Space: *Davis Creek Park Trail Map* (https://www.washoecounty.us/parks/files/trail_maps/Davis%20Creek%20Regional%20Park%20Trails%20Map%2011%20x%208%205.pdf)
MANAGEMENT	Washoe County Parks and Open Space at 775-328-3600, www.washoecounty.us/parks

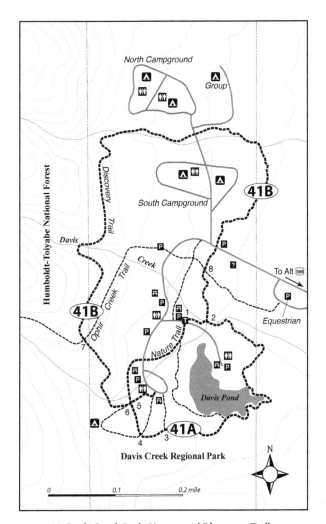

41. Davis Creek Park: Nature and Discovery Trails

HIGHLIGHTS Forest, interpretive brochure, pond

LOWLIGHTS The park may feel a bit crowded on summer weekends

TIP | The park is much quieter in the off-season.

KID TIP | Davis Creek Park is well suited for family visits. With picnic areas, a campground, fishing and swimming in Davis Pond, and various recreational facilities, along with the trails, a family could easily spend a day, weekend, or several days here. With brochure in hand, the Nature Trail would be a fine way to introduce some of the natural environment to young children.

Bridge across stream in Davis Creek Park

TRAILHEAD ⏐ 39°18.214′W, 119°49.993′W From Carson City, follow I-580 northbound toward Reno. Take Exit 50 and follow signs for Davis Creek Park, turning left from the off-ramp and immediately turning right again into the park entrance. Follow the park road past the equestrian trailhead, park head-quarters, campground entrance, and Ophir Creek trailhead to a junction with a road on the left. Turn left down this road, and drive a short distance to the parking area on the left. The trail begins at the far end of the parking area, marked by a sign with a Jeffrey pinecone, which is the trail's symbol.

TRAIL ⏐ Grab a copy of the *Davis Creek Naturalist Guide* from a box at the trail-head **[1]** and head east through typical sagebrush scrub vegetation, including bitterbrush and sagebrush, with a smattering of Jeffrey pines. Near post 1, you soon reach a junction **[2]** with the Discovery Trail heading left (north) and the combined route of the Nature Trail and Discovery Trail on the right.

Continuing east, the Nature Trail drops to a bridge crossing over an alder-lined seasonal stream. Beyond the bridge, the trail meanders up and around an open hillside carpeted with sagebrush scrub with fine views of Washoe Valley backdropped by the brown-tinged peaks of the Virginia Range. Bending south, the path leads into Jeffrey pine forest and past a picnic area to the northeast shore of Davis Pond. Across the pond's surface is a good view of towering Slide Mountain. The trail passes by fences separating the park from private residences to the east. Pass around the south shore of Davis Pond and head east through the trees. Reach an unmarked junction [3] with a path on the right from the Lakeview Picnic Area. Proceed ahead to where an old road comes in from the south parking area just before a bridge over a ditch carrying water from Ophir Creek to the pond and a junction [4] immediately beyond.

Turn right at the junction, and follow the ditch for a while, soon intersecting a set of wood-berm stairs. [5] While the Discovery Trail heads uphill to the left, the path to the right leads shortly to the south parking area. Continue ahead on the Nature Trail on a short descent across a culvert and past a picnic area to a crosswalk over the park's access road. Pick up the trail again on the far side and follow gently graded tread past some tall shrubs to a railed bridge. Past the bridge, the trail travels shortly past post 10 and closes the loop at the parking area. [1]

DAVIS POND Although originally a naturally occurring body of water, Davis Pond has been enhanced over the years to its current size of 2.5 acres and fifteen-foot depth. Fed by waters from Davis Creek and a ditch from Ophir Creek to the south, the pond is usually full except in late summer following drier-than-average winters. NDOW stocks the pond with rainbow trout in the spring and late summer (three-per-day limit). When winter conditions are favorable, Davis Pond is open for free ice-skating.

In the latter 1800s, the pond was used by the Winters Ranch for gathering ice to be used at their mansion and for sale to the residents of Virginia City during the mining heyday. Built in 1863, the mansion was added to the National Register of Historic Places in 1974. Located at the northwest end of Washoe Valley, the mansion is clearly visible on the east side of Old US 395, just south of Winters Creek.

MILESTONES
1: Start at Nature Trail trailhead; 2: Right at Discovery Trail junction; 3: Straight at junction; 4: Right at ditch junction; 5: Straight at Nature Trail junction; 1: Reach trailhead.

Davis Pond in autumn

41B ▪ Discovery Trail

LEVEL	Walk, intermediate
LENGTH	1.9 miles, loop
TIME	1 to 2 hours
ELEVATION	+175′/−175′
USERS	Hikers, trail runners, mountain bikers
DOGS	On leash

Moon above the Carson Range from the Discovery Trail

DIFFICULTY	Moderate
SEASON	April to December
BEST TIME	May through June
FACILITIES	Campground, fishing, horseshoe pits, picnic areas, restrooms, volleyball area
MAP	Washoe County Parks and Open Space: *Davis Creek Park Trail Map* (https://www.washoecounty.us/parks/files/trail_maps/Davis%20Creek%20Regional%20Park%20Trails%20Map%2011%20x%208%205.pdf)
MANAGEMENT	Washoe County Parks and Open Space at 775-328-3600, www.washoecounty.us/parks
HIGHLIGHTS	Forest, pond, stream
LOWLIGHTS	The park may feel a bit crowded on summer weekends

TIP | The park is much quieter in the off-season.

KID TIP | Davis Creek Park is well suited for family visits. With picnic areas, a campground, fishing and swimming in Davis Pond, and recreational facilities, along with the trails, a family could easily spend a day, a weekend, or several days here.

TRAILHEAD | 39°18.214′W, 119°49.993′W From Carson City, follow I-580 northbound toward Reno. Take Exit 50 and follow signs for Davis Creek Park, turning left from the off-ramp and immediately turning right again into the park entrance. Follow the park road past the equestrian trailhead, park headquarters, campground entrance, and Ophir Creek trailhead to a junction with a road on the left. Turn left down this road and drive a short distance to the parking area on the left. The trail begins at the far end of the parking area, marked by a sign with a Jeffrey pinecone, which is the Nature Trail's symbol.

TRAIL | From the trailhead, go east through typical sagebrush scrub vegetation, including bitterbrush and sagebrush, with a smattering of Jeffrey pines. Near post 1, you soon reach a junction [2] with the Discovery Trail heading left (north) and the combined route of the Nature Trail and Discovery Trail on the right.

Continuing east, the Nature Trail drops to a bridge crossing over an alder-lined seasonal stream. Beyond the bridge, the trail meanders up and around an open hillside carpeted with sagebrush scrub with fine views of Washoe Valley backdropped by the brown peaks of the Virginia Range. Bending south, the path leads into Jeffrey pine forest and past a picnic area to the northeast shore of Davis Pond. Across the pond's surface is a good view of towering Slide Mountain. The trail passes by fences separating the park from private residences to the east. Pass around the south shore of Davis Pond and head east through the trees. Reach an unmarked junction [3] with a path on the right from the Lakeview Picnic Area. Proceed ahead to where an old road comes in from the south parking area just before a bridge over a ditch carrying water from Ophir Creek to the pond and a junction [4] immediately beyond.

Turn right at the junction and follow the ditch for a while, soon intersecting a set of wood-berm stairs, [5] 0.6 mile from the trailhead.

Leaving the shared course with the Nature Trail, turn left and climb up the slope a very short way to a Y junction [6] with a path on the left leading to the group tent area. Veer onto the right-hand trail climbing alongside and then crossing a gully. Continue the ascent across a couple more usually dry gullies to a junction [7] with the wide track of the Ophir Creek Trail at 0.8 mile. Go straight here, climbing into more open forest, which allows a patchy understory of sagebrush, bitterbrush, and manzanita. Eventually the grade eases, as you follow a gently descending traverse across the hillside. Bend into the narrow, aspen-lined canyon of perennial Davis Creek. Cross the creek on a short wood bridge and continue away from the creek on a traverse across the forested slope before a brief descent leads to the narrow swale of a seasonal stream. The trail bends and follows the south bank of this creek downstream. (Ignore a side trail coming in on the left from the campground.) Where the swale flattens out, you cross to the far bank and continue downstream to the campground access road, 1.4 miles from the trailhead.

Follow a crosswalk across the road and back onto single-track tread, just to the right of a gravel road to the group camp area. You emerge out of the Jeffrey pine forest and wind around through sagebrush scrub, enjoying views across Washoe Valley to the Virginia Range. Nearing the edge of park property at a barbed-wire fence, the trail bends south and heads toward the main park access road. Just before reaching the road, the trail passes above an overflow parking lot. After crossing the road, you reach a junction [8] with the equestrian access to the Ophir Creek Trail.

Proceed ahead from the junction and wind around to the Nature Trail junction [2] at the close of the loop. From there, retrace your steps to the nearby parking area. [1]

MILESTONES

1: Start at Nature Trail trailhead; 2: Right at Discovery Trail junction; 3: Straight at junction; 4: Right at ditch junction; 5: Left at Nature Trail junction; 6: Right at Y junction; 7: Straight at Ophir Creek junction; 8: Straight at equestrian trail junction; 2: Right at Nature Trail junction; 1: Return to trailhead.

GO GREEN | Washoe County Parks and Open Space has an Adopt-A-Park program, where volunteers can donate their time for "hands-on work in our parks, helping to keep them clean, attractive and safe for everyone to enjoy." The program is open to individuals and groups. For more information, visit their website and click on the link for the Adopt-A-Park program, or contact the Parks volunteer coordinator at 775-785-4512, ext. 107.

OPTIONS | Although without significant trails, two other parks nearby are worth visiting, Bowers Mansion and Wilson Commons. There has been discussion about a trail one day connecting Davis Creek and Bowers Mansion.

Washoe Lake State Park: Little Washoe Lake

A short walk along the southeast shore of Little Washoe Lake is an easy jaunt from the trailhead to wetlands in the Scripps Wildlife Management Area near the north end of much larger Washoe Lake. A wide variety of migratory birds and waterfowl make use of the wetlands habitat for foraging and nesting. Birds you might see in this area include pelicans, herons, and ibis. Pairs of bald eagles winter in this area occasionally, and red-tailed hawks are more common year-round residents. A bird checklist is available from park headquarters for avid birdwatchers. The open terrain around Little Washoe Lake also allows for fine views of the Carson Range to the west and the Virginia Range to the east.

LEVEL	Walk, novice
LENGTH	1.0 mile, out and back
TIME	1/2 to 1 hour
ELEVATION	Negligible
USERS	Hikers, equestrians
DOGS	On leash
DIFFICULTY	Easy
SEASON	March through November
BEST TIME	April through May
FACILITIES	Vault toilets at trailhead, boat launch, campground, picnic areas, restrooms, showers
MAPS	Nevada State Parks (NSP): *Washoe Lake State Park* (web map); USGS: *Carson City*
MANAGEMENT	Washoe Lake State Park at 775-687-4319, www.parks.nv .gov/parks/washoe-lake-state-park/
HIGHLIGHTS	Lake, views, wildlife
LOWLIGHTS	Exposed to sun, fee

TRAILHEAD | 39°19.570'N, 119°47.533'W From Carson City, follow I-580 north to the Old US 395 Exit 50, and head north on ALT 395 for 3 miles to a right-hand turn onto Eastlake Boulevard. Head south on Eastlake for about one hundred yards, and turn right at the entrance to the parking area

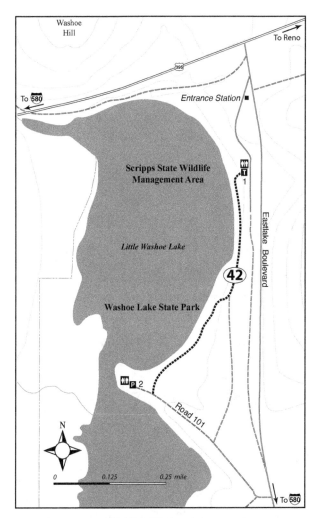

42. Little Washoe Lake

for Little Washoe Lake. Pay your day-use fee and self-register at the kiosk. Continue ahead and park your vehicle near the south end of the lot.

TRAIL | Single-track tread leads away from the south end of the parking lot, passing picnic areas on the way to where the trail merges with a dirt road. Following signs toward the lakeshore, you travel southwest along the shoreline of Little Washoe Lake, with fine views of Mt. Rose, Slide Mountain, and the Carson Range to the west. Approaching the south end of Little Washoe Lake, the route merges with a gravel road on the way west to a parking lot [2]

Little Washoe Lake and the Carson Range

White-faced Ibis

(vault toilets) near the channel between Little Washoe and Washoe Lakes. Retrace your steps to the starting trailhead. [1]

> **WHITE-FACED IBIS** (*Plegadis chihi*) Widespread in the United States across the west, central, and southeast states, the white-faced ibis—a long-legged, dark-colored, wading bird with a down-curved bill—prefers shallow, freshwater marshes for their diet of mostly insects. They migrate to such areas as Washoe Lake to breed in colonies, typically building nests in bushes or low trees. This species was added to the Migratory Bird Treaty Act of 1918 when studies indicated the pesticide DDT was affecting their eggshells. Additional threats include pollution and habitat destruction.

MILESTONES

1: Start at Little Washoe Lake trailhead; **2:** South parking area; **1:** Return to trailhead.

GO GREEN | Muscle Powered is the preeminent organization for building and maintaining trails in Carson City. Established in 1999, the group has been an unparalleled advocate for biking and hiking trails in the area. Along with trail building and maintenance, education, and advocacy, the nonprofit group also hosts community events. They routinely sponsor trash mobs, cleanup projects that provide a valuable asset to the beautification of the greater Carson City area. You can become a member and support the work at www .musclepowered.org.

OPTIONS | The campground at Washoe Lake State Park would be a fine place to spend a night or two, especially if the water level is suitable for boating.

Beginning on the historic Jumbo Grade road, this route veers away on a steep climb to the top of a peak known locally as Jumbo Hill. The top offers a sweeping view across Washoe Valley of a large section of the Carson Range.

LEVEL	Hike, advanced
LENGTH	2.8 miles, Loop
TIME	1-1/2 hours
ELEVATION	+900'/–900'
USERS	Hikers, trail runners, mountain bikers, equestrians
DOGS	OK
DIFFICULTY	Strenuous
SEASON	All year
BEST TIMES	Spring, fall
FACILITIES	Horse loading area, interpretive signs, vault toilets
MAP	USGS: *Virginia City*
MANAGEMENT	Bureau of Land Management at 775-861-6400, www.blm.gov/nv/st/en/fo/carson_city_field.html
HIGHLIGHTS	Views, wildlife
LOWLIGHTS	Exposed to sun, rough trails, no signage, numerous trails and roads, open to OHVs

TIP | Get an early start in the summer to beat the heat. Bring plenty of water and sunscreen. Visit on a weekday to hopefully avoid too much OHV traffic.

KID TIP | Younger children will probably dislike the steep and exposed climb.

TRAILHEAD | 39°16.886′N, 119°44.356′W From Carson City, follow I-580 north to the Eastlake Boulevard Exit 44, and make a right-hand turn onto Eastlake Boulevard. Head north on Eastlake for 6.4 miles to a right-hand turn onto Jumbo Grade Way. Proceed for another mile to the signed entrance to the Jumbo Grade trailhead and staging area.

TRAIL | From the trailhead, follow a path downhill along a fence to rejoin the dirt track of Jumbo Grade Way. Turning upstream, you follow the main road up the canyon. Just shy of a quarter mile, leave Jumbo Grade and veer left at a Y junction [2] onto a road that immediately crosses the creek and

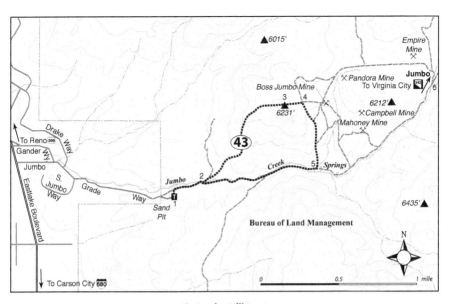

43. Jumbo Hill Loop

Slide Mountain and Mt. Rose from the Jumbo Hill Loop

Great Basin Gopher Snake

then climbs moderately steeply up the hillside. Continue ascending across slopes covered by dry, sagebrush scrub with a smattering of spring wildflowers. The steady ascent is interrupted briefly on a dip into a seasonal swale before the stiff climb resumes. Farther on, the grade eases momentarily when the old road passes to the south of a knoll, where a few Utah junipers appear. Continue to the flat-topped summit of Jumbo Hill. [3] The fine view from the top includes many Carson Range peaks, such as Slide Mountain, Mt. Rose, Snow Valley Peak, Jobs Peak, Jobs Sister, and Freel Peak. To the east is a good vista of the rolling hills of the Virginia Range.

Heading east, make a steep, rough, and rocky descent from the summit to a four-way junction. [4] Turn right and head downslope, passing a couple of junctions with other roads on the way to a T junction [5] with Jumbo Grade near a spring.

Turn right again at the junction, heading generally west along Jumbo Grade, following the course of Jumbo Creek. Reach the Y junction [2] at the close of the loop, and then retrace your steps to the trailhead. [1]

GREAT BASIN GOPHER SNAKE (*Pituophis catenifer deserticola*) Sometimes confused with the western rattlesnake in northern Nevada, the nonvenomous Great Basin gopher snake has the ability to mimic its poisonous counterpart by flattening its head to a triangular shape and inflating its body to appear larger. Furthering the confusion, the gopher snake can also imitate the sound of the rattle by vibrating its tail in dry vegetation or loose gravel. These snakes are also referred to as bull snakes.

MILESTONES

1: Start at Jumbo Grade trailhead; 2: Veer left at Y junction; 3: Top of Jumbo Hill; 4: Turn right at four-way junction; 5: Turn right at T junction; 2: Go straight at Y junction; 1: Return to trailhead.

GO GREEN I Muscle Powered is the preeminent organization for building and maintaining trails in Carson City. Established in 1999, the group has been an unparalleled advocate for biking and hiking trails in the area. Along with trail building and maintenance, education, and advocacy, the nonprofit group also hosts community events. They routinely sponsor trash mobs, cleanup projects that provide a valuable asset to the beautification of the greater Carson City area. You can become a member and support the work at www .musclepowered.org.

OPTIONS I So many roads and trails crisscross this area that finding alternate routes is virtually limitless.

Jumbo Townsite

On this trip travelers can journey through history on the old Jumbo Grade road to the abandoned townsite of Jumbo, which served a community of miners who prospected in the neighboring hills. Along the way, fortunate travelers may see a herd of wild horses.

LEVEL	Hike, intermediate
LENGTH	4.5 miles, out and back
TIME	2 hours
ELEVATION	+650'/−25'
USERS	Hikers, trail runners, mountain bikers, equestrians
DOGS	OK
DIFFICULTY	Moderate
SEASON	All year
BEST TIMES	Spring, fall
FACILITIES	Horse loading area, interpretive signs, vault toilets
MAP	USGS: *Virginia City*
MANAGEMENT	Bureau of Land Management at 775-861-6400, www.blm .gov/nv/st/en/fo/carson_city_field.html
HIGHLIGHTS	History, wildlife
LOWLIGHTS	Exposed to sun, rough trails, no signage, numerous trails and roads, open to OHVs

TIP I Get an early start in the summer to beat the heat. Bring plenty of water and sunscreen. Visit on a weekday to avoid too much OHV traffic.

KID TIP I Many kids will probably enjoy the opportunity to poke around the old townsite.

TRAILHEAD I 39°16.886′N, 119°44.356′W From Carson City, follow I-580 north to the Eastlake Boulevard Exit 44 and make a right-hand turn onto Eastlake Boulevard. Head north on Eastlake for 6.4 miles to a right-hand turn onto Jumbo Grade Way. Proceed for another mile to the signed entrance to the Jumbo Grade trailhead and staging area.

TRAIL I From the trailhead, follow a path downhill along a fence to rejoin the dirt track of Jumbo Grade Way. Turning upstream, you follow the main

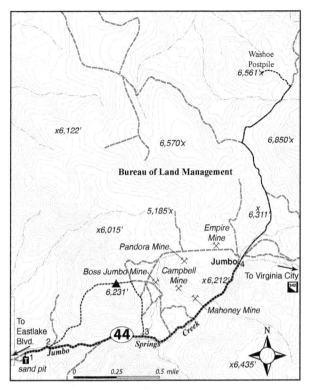

44. Jumbo Townsite

road up the canyon on a moderate ascent. Just shy of 0.25 mile, you reach a Y junction, [2] where the route of Trip 43 heads across the creek and steeply uphill. Continue ahead on Jumbo Grade, following the course of diminutive Jumbo Creek upstream through the canyon. Near the 1-mile mark in the vicinity of a spring, at a junction [3] a prominent road heads north up a drainage, but you continue ahead on the main road. Where the canyon bends northeast, reach another spring that feeds water into the creek. Remain on Jumbo Grade, clearly the most used road, as lesser roads seem to branch away with some regularity. The moderate climb intensifies for a short time in the vicinity of a steep hill. Farther on, the canyon narrows for a while until widening out again near where the road crosses the streambed, which is usually dry at this point. Keep climbing to the old townsite, [4] reaching a major junction at 2.25 miles, where Jumbo Grade turns east and continues toward Virginia City. Once your explorations are complete, retrace your steps to the trailhead. [1]

Old pit near Jumbo Townsite

JUMBO (TOWNSITE) About the only thing that could accurately be described as jumbo in this area were the aspirations of the miners, as their mines never produced all that much valuable ore. Before the town existed, Ophir Grade (eventually renamed Jumbo Grade) was built to connect the much more lucrative mines of Virginia City to the Ophir Mill on the shore of Washoe Lake. At one time, this quartz mill employed around one hundred workers and occupied a site over an acre in size before closing around 1866. During its heyday in the early 1900s, the town of Jumbo had a mill, saloons, hotels, shops, and a post office. Once the mines had played out, the town was abandoned by 1921.

MILESTONES

1: Start at Jumbo Grade trailhead; **2:** Straight at Y junction; **3:** Straight at junction; **4:** Jumbo townsite; **1:** Return to trailhead.

GO GREEN ǀ Muscle Powered is the preeminent organization for building and maintaining trails in Carson City. Established in 1999, the group has been an unparalleled advocate for biking and hiking trails in the area. Along with trail building and maintenance, education, and advocacy, the nonprofit group also hosts community events. They routinely sponsor trash mobs, cleanup projects that provide a valuable asset to the beautification of the greater Carson City area. You can become a member and support the work at www .musclepowered.org.

OPTIONS ǀ So many roads and trails crisscross this area that finding alternate routes is virtually limitless. One very interesting but longer extension continues northbound on a road for a mile to a Y intersection. From there, take the right-hand road another 0.6 mile to where a faint jeep track heads northwest toward point 6561. Follow the faint track to the end, and continue cross-country to the top, 0.25 mile from the road, where you will find Washoe Postpile, an andesite formation similar in appearance to the much more renowned Devils Postpile near Mammoth Lakes, California.

Washoe Lake State Park: Loop Trails

Along with a 3-mile paved bike path and miles of old roads on the east side, Washoe Lake State Park has several designated trails to offer excursions for a wide range of recreationists. Of those, four loop trails, from 1.1 miles to 3.8 miles are described below. The North, East, and South Loops travel through the sagebrush scrub terrain to the east of the lake, while the Wetlands Loop wanders through a man-made wetlands at the south end.

When the freeway was constructed through Washoe Valley many years ago, some of the area's wetlands were altered. The Nevada Department of Transportation built a series of dikes at the south end of Washoe Lake to create new wetlands to compensate for this loss. A one-mile loop trail was designated along a portion of the gravel roads that run along the top of these dikes, along with an elevated observation deck, to provide opportunities for hikers and naturalists to observe the abundant wildlife inhabiting this area. Between February 1 and July 15, you must stick to the designated route so as not to disturb any nesting birds. During drought cycles, when the lake is below the level to allow water into the wetlands, this trip loses much of its appeal. However, the fine views of the valley bordered by the Carson Range to the west and the Virginia Range to the east are always excellent.

45A ▪ North Loop

LEVEL	Walk, novice
LENGTH	3.4 miles, loop
TIME	1-1/2 to 2 hours
ELEVATION	Negligible
USERS	Hikers, trail runners, mountain bikers, equestrians
DOGS	OK (on leash within 200 feet of camping/picnic areas)
DIFFICULTY	Easy
SEASON	All year
BEST TIME	April through May
FACILITIES	Vault toilets and interpretive signs at trailhead, boat launch, campground, picnic areas, restrooms, showers

MAPS NSP: *Washoe Lake State Park* (http://parks.nv.gov/forms /washoe_trail_map.pdf); USGS: *Carson City*

MANAGEMENT Washoe Lake State Park at 775-687-4319, www.parks.nv .gov/parks/washoe-lake-state-park/

HIGHLIGHTS Lake, wildlife

LOWLIGHTS Exposed to sun

TIP | Get an early start when temperatures are forecasted to be hot, as there is absolutely no shade along the entire route.

KID TIP | These easy loop hikes are fine for kids, but the high usage by equestrians suggests keeping the little ones close at hand.

TRAILHEAD | 39°16.566′N, 119°47.249′W From Carson City, follow I-580 north to the Old US 395 Exit 50, and head north on ALT 395 for 3 miles to a right-hand turn onto Eastlake Boulevard. Head south on Eastlake for 2.1 miles, and turn right at Lakeshore Drive. Proceed 1.8 miles toward Douglas Drive, and just before the intersection, turn right onto County Road 233 (signed for the boat ramp); then drive a short distance to the trailhead parking area on the left-hand side of the road.

TRAIL | The North Loop heads southeast away from the trailhead briefly and then heads east along Ormsby Lane to the end before angling southeast again. At a junction [2] with the East Loop, the trail travels south to a junction [3] with the South Loop, arcs to the west briefly to the next junction, [4] and then turns northwest on the way back to the trailhead. [1]

MILESTONES

1: Start at equestrian trailhead; **2:** Veer right at East Loop junction; **3:** Turn right at South Loop junction; **4:** Turn right at junction; **1:** Return to trailhead.

GO GREEN | Muscle Powered is the preeminent organization for building and maintaining trails in Carson City. Established in 1999, the group has been an unparalleled advocate for biking and hiking trails in the area. Along with trail building and maintenance, education, and advocacy, the nonprofit group also hosts community events. They routinely sponsor trash mobs, cleanup projects that provide a valuable asset to the beautification of the greater Carson City area. You can become a member and support the work at www .musclepowered.org.

OPTIONS | Every day but Monday you can grab a pre-hike breakfast or a post-hike lunch at the Postal Café, which occupies an old gas station at 3115 Eastlake Boulevard in the small commercial center of Washoe Valley. Although the menu is typical diner fare, the food is fresh and well prepared.

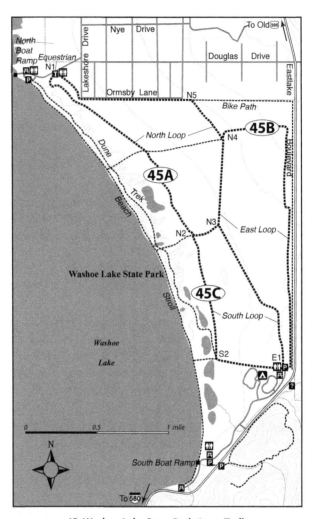

45. Washoe Lake State Park: Loop Trails

45B ▪ East Loop

LEVEL	Walk, novice
LENGTH	3.8 miles, loop
TIME	2 hours
ELEVATION	Negligible
USERS	Hikers, trail runners, mountain bikers, equestrians
DOGS	OK (on leash within 200 feet of camping/picnic areas)
DIFFICULTY	Easy
SEASON	March to December

BEST TIME	April through May
FACILITIES	Vault toilets and interpretive signs at trailhead, boat launch, campground, picnic areas, restrooms, showers
MAPS	NSP: *Washoe Lake State Park* (http://parks.nv.gov/forms /washoe_trail_map.pdf); USGS: *Carson City*
MANAGEMENT	Washoe Lake State Park at 775-687-4319, www.parks.nv .gov/parks/washoe-lake-state-park/
HIGHLIGHTS	Lake, wildlife
LOWLIGHTS	Exposed to sun

TIP | Get an early start when temperatures are forecasted to be hot, as there is absolutely no shade along the entire route.

KID TIP | These easy loop hikes are fine for kids, but the high usage by equestrians suggests keeping the little ones close at hand.

TRAILHEAD | 39°14.838′N, 119°45.503′W From Carson City, follow I-580 north to the Eastlake Boulevard Exit 44, and head northeast on Eastlake for 3.2 miles to a left-hand turn, signed for the campground. Turn right and continue past the campground to the equestrian parking area.

TRAIL | Follow the wide track of the right-hand roadbed away from the parking area, and head north for 0.3 mile on the shared track of the East and South Loops to a junction. [2] Turn left for a short distance where the route bends northwest. After 0.7 mile you come to a junction [3] with the North Loop and turn right on the shared course of the East and North Loops heading northbound. Reach another junction [4] after 0.6 mile, where the North Loop angles to the northwest, but you turn right to travel north-northeast on a single-track trail toward Eastlake Boulevard. After 0.4 mile, [5] the route bends south to roughly parallel the road on the way back toward the trailhead, which is 1.8 miles away. Just before the trailhead, the trail crosses a dirt road and arcs around to the parking area. [1]

MILESTONES
1: Start at trailhead; 2: Turn left at junction; 3: Turn right at North Loop junction; 4: Turn right at junction; 5: Turn south; 1: Return to trailhead.

45C ▪ South Loop

LEVEL	Walk, novice
LENGTH	2.5 miles, loop
TIME	1 hour
ELEVATION	Negligible
USERS	Hikers, trail runners, mountain bikers, equestrians
DOGS	OK (on leash within 200 feet of camping/picnic areas)
DIFFICULTY	Easy

Clouds above Washoe Lake

SEASON March to December

BEST TIME April through May

FACILITIES Vault toilets and interpretive signs at trailhead, boat launch, campground, picnic areas, restrooms, showers

MAPS NSP: *Washoe Lake State Park* (http://parks.nv.gov/forms /washoe_trail_map.pdf); USGS: *Carson City*

MANAGEMENT Washoe Lake State Park at 775-687-4319, www.parks.nv .gov/parks/washoe-lake-state-park/

HIGHLIGHTS Lake, wildlife

LOWLIGHTS Exposed to sun

TIP ꞯ Get an early start when temperatures are forecasted to be hot, as there is absolutely no shade along the entire route.

KID TIP ꞯ These easy loop hikes are fine for kids, but the high usage by equestrians suggests keeping the little ones close at hand.

TRAILHEAD ꞯ 39°14.838′N, 119°45.503′W From Carson City, follow I-580 north to the Eastlake Boulevard Exit 44, and head northeast on Eastlake for 3.2 miles to a left-hand turn, signed for the campground. Turn right and continue past the campground to the equestrian parking area.

TRAIL ꞯ Follow the wide track of the right-hand roadbed away from the parking area, and head north for 0.3 mile on the shared track of the East and South Loops to a junction. [2] Turn left for a short distance where the route bends northwest. After 0.7 mile you come to a junction [3] with the North

Loop and turn left. After 0.2 mile you reach a four-way junction, [4] where the North Loop heads northwest, the path ahead goes to the lakeshore, and the South Loop turns southeast. Turning left, you travel generally south-bound for 0.9 mile to the next junction. [5] Turn sharply left here and proceed east for 0.4 mile back to the trailhead. [1]

MILESTONES

1: Start at trailhead; 2: Turn left at junction; 3: Turn left at North Loop junction; 4: Turn left at junction; 5: Turn left at junction; 1: Return to trailhead.

45D ▪ Wetlands Loop

LEVEL	Walk, novice
LENGTH	1.1 miles, lollipop loop
TIME	1 hour
ELEVATION	Negligible
USERS	Hikers
DOGS	OK (on leash within 200 feet of camping/picnic areas)
DIFFICULTY	Easy
SEASON	March to December
BEST TIME	April through May
FACILITIES	Vault toilets and interpretive signs at trailhead, boat launch, campground, picnic areas, restrooms, showers
MAPS	NSP: *Washoe Lake State Park* (http://parks.nv.gov/forms /washoe_trail_map.pdf); USGS: *Carson City*
MANAGEMENT	Washoe Lake State Park at 775-687-4319, www.parks.nv .gov/parks/washoe-lake-state-park/
HIGHLIGHTS	Views, wildlife
LOWLIGHTS	Lack of water during drought cycles, exposed to sun

TIP ǀ There is virtually no shade on this loop, so during the summer months, get an early start if you want to beat the heat.

KID TIP ǀ When the water level is high enough in Washoe Lake to provide water to the wetlands, kids should find this hike to be quite entertaining with the bountiful wildlife. When the water level is too low, looking for another hike in the area might be a good bet.

TRAILHEAD ǀ 39°13.610′N, 119°47.567′W. From Carson City, follow I-580 north to the Lakeview Exit 44, and head east on Eastlake Boulevard. Continue for 1.3 miles to a left-hand turn into the signed parking area.

TRAIL ǀ The trail begins on the east side of the parking area and follows a split-railed fence toward Washoe Lake. Reach a junction [2] just before the raised observation deck, which provides an elevated vantage from where to

A split-rail fence lines part of the Wetlands Loop at the south end of Washoe Lake

Osprey nest

scan the wetlands for the abundant birdlife, at least when the lake is high enough to feed water into the area. Interpretive signs offer interesting bits of information about the wetlands and its residents.

At the junction, turn right and head east for a short way to another junction [3] marked by a four-by-four post. Turn left and proceed toward the lake again, soon reaching a T intersection. [4] Turn left again and embark on a much longer walk, following a roadbed on top of an east-west dike and soon passing to the north of the observation deck. Farther on, you come to a four-way intersection [5] and turn left to continue the loop. Proceed southbound for 0.1 mile to the next junction. [6] Once again you make a left-hand turn and head back toward the observation deck [2] and the completion of the loop section. From there, retrace your steps to the trailhead. [1]

> **OSPREY** (*Pandion haliaetus*) This widely distributed raptor is found near bodies of water with adequate food supplies, their diets consisting mainly of fish. Along with owls, the osprey is the only other raptor species with reversible outer toes, which allow them to grasp slippery fish with two toes in front and behind. In flight, ospreys can be identified by their short tails and long and skinny, arched, mostly white (underside) wings comprised of four long feathers and a shorter fifth feather. These birds typically mate for life, with females bearing two to four eggs.

MILESTONES

1: Start at Wetlands Loop trailhead; **2:** Turn left at junction; **3:** Turn right at observation deck junction; **4:** Turn left at junction; **5:** Turn left at junction; **6:** Turn left at junction; **2:** Turn right at observation deck junction; **1:** Return to trailhead.

GO GREEN | Muscle Powered is the preeminent organization for building and maintaining trails in Carson City. Established in 1999, the group has been an unparalleled advocate for biking and hiking trails in the area. Along with trail building and maintenance, education, and advocacy, the nonprofit group also hosts community events. They routinely sponsor trash mobs, cleanup projects that provide a valuable asset to the beautification of the greater Carson City area. You can become a member and support the work at www.musclepowered.org.

OPTIONS | Look for an alternative hike when the water level is low. Trip 42 along the east shore of Little Washoe Lake is similar in distance and elevation gain/loss. Note: Trail not shown on map on page 236.

Washoe Lake State Park: Dune Trek–Beach Stroll Loop

Combining the Dune Trek with a section of the Beach Stroll allows hikers to create a loop trail providing two different perspectives of Washoe Lake's environment. Beginning with the Dune Trek, the route rolls across the sand dunes on the east side of the lake. The return follows along the lakeshore, affording good views of the surrounding terrain and the opportunity to see some of the many species of waterfowl that temporarily inhabit these waters.

LEVEL	Hike, intermediate
LENGTH	5.4 miles, loop
TIME	3 hours
ELEVATION	+100'/−100'
USERS	Hikers, trail runners, mountain bikers, equestrians
DOGS	OK (on leash within 200 feet of camping/picnic areas)
DIFFICULTY	Moderate
SEASON	March to December
BEST TIME	April to mid-June
FACILITIES	boat launch, picnic area, restrooms at trailhead, campground, showers nearby
MAPS	NSP: *Washoe Lake State Park* (http://parks.nv.gov/forms/washoe_trail_map.pdf); USGS: *Carson City*
MANAGEMENT	Washoe Lake State Park at 775-687-4319, www.parks.nv.gov/parks/washoe-lake-state-park/
HIGHLIGHTS	Lake, views, wildlife
LOWLIGHTS	Sandy tread

TIP | The deep sands through the dunes and along the lakeshore will make this a more strenuous trip compared to one of a similar length on compacted soils.

KID TIP | The beach sand will make travel a bit strenuous for small children. Rather than attempting to complete the entire loop, you may opt for a short stroll along the lakeshore to see some of the wildlife, followed by lunch at the picnic area.

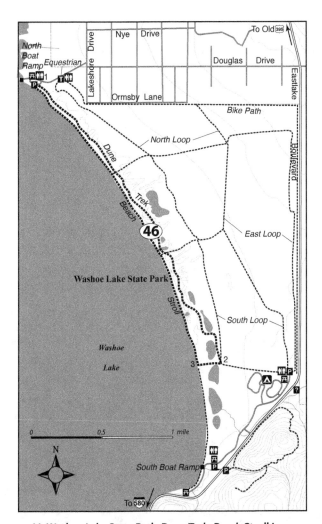

46. Washoe Lake State Park: Dune Trek–Beach Stroll Loop

TRAILHEAD | 39°16.523′N, 119°47.441′W From Carson City, follow I-580 north to the Old US 395 Exit 50, and head north on ALT 395 for 3 miles to a right-hand turn onto Eastlake Boulevard. Head south on Eastlake for 2.1 miles, and turn right at Lakeshore Drive. Proceed 1.8 miles toward Douglas Drive; just before the intersection, turn right onto County Road 233 (signed for the boat ramp) and then drive into the park. After stopping at the entrance station to pay your fee, continue to the parking lot near the picnic area.

TRAIL | The trail begins across from the picnic area in an area of sand. Without the aid of defined tread, locate a four-by-four post with detailed trail

A section of the dunes at Washoe Lake

information for the Dune Trek. Head south-southeast across the dunes, where a lack of vegetation to hold the soil in place allows the wind to continuously redistribute the sand and thereby prevent the establishment of a distinct trail. Widely spaced four-by-four posts may help keep you on track, and despite the lack of defined tread, the open terrain and landmark of the lakeshore will keep you from getting lost. The increase of scrubby vegetation farther on, including sagebrush, bitterbrush, and ephedra, allows for a more

American White Pelican

established tread for the majority of the remaining hike along the Dune Trek portion. Along the way, you must negotiate minor ups and downs, as the route periodically crests low dunes and drops into shallow drainages. The view of Washoe Lake comes and goes but the Carson Range to the west and Virginia Range to the east remain in sight the entire way.

Near the two-mile mark, the route dips into a deep draw, bends to the east briefly, and then skirts to the west of a shallow pond/meadow. At the far end, the trail veers east again shortly before adopting a southeasterly course across the dunes. About a quarter mile farther, you reach a junction [2] with the lateral from the campground.

Turn right (west) at the junction and head toward Washoe Lake. Reach the lakeshore [3] after 0.2 mile and turn right again. From there, follow the shoreline for 1.5 miles back to the trailhead.

AMERICAN WHITE PELICAN (*Pelecanyus erythrorhynchos*) Pelicans are some of the largest birds in North America, with white bodies and broad, black-fringed wings. Their distinctive appearance comes from their large yellow-orange bills and big heads. These birds are surface feeders, dipping their beaks into the water to catch fish, consuming around four pounds per day. Pelicans typically nest as pairs in large colonies, females laying a clutch of two or three eggs per season.

MILESTONES

1: Start at North Boat Ramp trailhead; 2: Turn right at junction; 3: Turn right at lakeshore; 1: End at trailhead.

GO GREEN I Muscle Powered is the preeminent organization for building and maintaining trails in Carson City. Established in 1999, the group has been an unparalleled advocate for biking and hiking trails in the area. Along with trail building and maintenance, education, and advocacy, the nonprofit group also hosts community events. They routinely sponsor trash mobs, cleanup projects that provide a valuable asset to the beautification of the greater Carson City area. You can become a member and support the work at www .musclepowered.org.

OPTIONS I The open terrain allows for opportunities to easily shorten the hike if desired.

Deadman Creek Loop

Spring brings comfortable temperatures and colorful wildflowers to the Deadman Creek Loop, particularly on the initial stretch along the lushly lined creek. Beyond the creek, a climb across open slopes covered in sagebrush scrub offers fine views of Washoe Lake and the peaks of the Carson and Virginia Ranges.

LEVEL	Hike, intermediate
LENGTH	1.3 miles, out and back to viewpoint; 2.4 miles, loop
TIME	1 hour to viewpoint and back; 1 to 2 hours for loop
ELEVATION	+300'/−300'; +500'/−500'
USERS	Hikers, trail runners, mountain bikers, equestrians
DOGS	OK
DIFFICULTY	Moderate
SEASON	March through October
BEST TIME	April through May
FACILITIES	No facilities at trailhead, boat launch, campground, picnic areas, restrooms, showers
MAPS	NSP: *Washoe Lake State Park* (http://parks.nv.gov/forms /washoe_trail_map.pdf); USGS: *Carson City*
MANAGEMENT	Washoe Lake State Park at 775-687-4319, www.parks.nv .gov/parks/washoe-lake-state-park/; Bureau of Land Management at 775-861-6400, www.blm.gov/nv/st/en/fo/carson_city _field.html
HIGHLIGHTS	Stream, views, wildflowers
LOWLIGHTS	Exposed to sun, poorly signed route beyond the creek, rattlesnakes

TIP I There is virtually no shade on this loop, so during the summer months, get an early start if you want to beat the heat. A number of social trails have evolved over the years, but the main trail appears as the most used path.

KID TIP I Small children will probably be best served by an out-and-back trip along Deadman Creek rather than the full loop across dry and open slopes. Kids should be fascinated by the water and riparian environment.

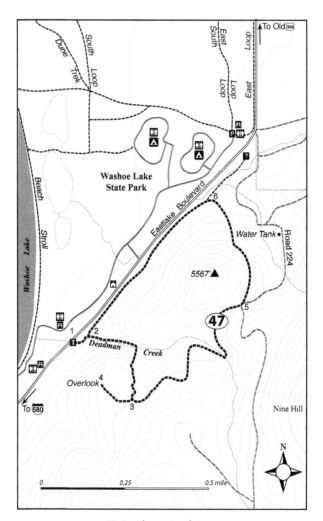

47. Deadman Creek Loop

TRAILHEAD | 39°14.301′N, 119°45.991′W From Carson City, follow I-580 north to the Lakeview Exit 44 and turn right onto Eastlake Boulevard. Continue for 3 miles to a small parking area on the right-hand shoulder.

TRAIL | From the trailhead, the Deadman Creek Trail climbs past a map and some metal interpretive markers, soon reaching a bridge across the usually dry streambed to the unmarked loop junction. [2] Veer to the right and keep ascending along the left-hand bank of the spring-fed section of the creek, where the lush riparian vegetation near the stream contrasts sharply with the drought-tolerant vegetation carpeting the hillsides. Above the spring,

Spring storm over Washoe Lake

the creek becomes seasonal again, as you continue up the drainage. Pass by a pair of side trails that cross the creek, and then reach a junction **[3]** at 0.3 mile with a lateral on the right heading toward an overlook with a view of Washoe Valley and the neighboring mountains.

Turn right at the junction and climb steadily for another 0.3 mile across an open slope to the top of a bench and a metal gazebo with a trio of short benches. After enjoying the fine vista, retrace your steps to the junction. **[3]** If you're just doing the out-and-back hike, retrace your steps to the trailhead. (You can vary your return slightly by turning left at the upper junction with the path that crosses the creek on a wood bridge and heading downstream to the lower bridge, beyond which you rejoin the main trail.)

For the full loop, turn right and travel generally northeast on a twisting and rolling climb across the slope through the wrinkled topography below

Nine Hill. On reaching a saddle, [4] the trail momentarily merges with the dirt surface of Road 224 before single track bends away to the north at a curve.

A gently graded traverse bends around the sagebrush-covered slopes of Peak 5,567 before switchbacks descend more steeply toward Eastlake Boulevard, reaching a junction [5] at the base of the hill.

Turn left and head southwest, paralleling the road on the way back to the junction at the close of the loop. [2] From there, retrace your steps a short way to the trailhead. [1]

GREAT BASIN RATTLESNAKE (*Crotalus oreganus lutosus*) A subspecies of the western rattlesnake, the brownish-patterned Great Basin rattlesnake reaches 1.5 to 4 feet in length at maturity. They have a triangular-shaped head and the characteristic rattle at the tail. Their diet consists primarily of amphibians, reptiles, birds, eggs, and small mammals. Although their bites are poisonous to humans, these snakes are not aggressive and will preferentially flee the presence of humans unless all escape routes are blocked. Their first line of defense is to remain motionless in hopes their camouflage coloring will keep them from being detected. If humans come too close, they will oftentimes give an audible warning with their rattles. Reserving their venom for prey, rattlesnakes are reluctant to bite humans.

MILESTONES (FULL LOOP)

1: Start at Deadman Creek trailhead; **2:** Turn right at junction; **3:** Overlook junction; **4:** Overlook; **3:** Overlook junction; **5:** Saddle, Road 224; **6:** Turn left at junction; **2:** Turn right at junction; **1:** Return to trailhead.

GO GREEN | Muscle Powered is the preeminent organization for building and maintaining trails in Carson City. Established in 1999, the group has been an unparalleled advocate for biking and hiking trails in the area. Along with trail building and maintenance, education, and advocacy, the nonprofit group also hosts community events. They routinely sponsor trash mobs, cleanup projects that provide a valuable asset to the beautification of the greater Carson City area. You can become a member and support the work at www .musclepowered.org.

OPTIONS | The campground at Washoe Lake State Park would be a fine place to spend a night or two, especially if the water level is suitable for boating.

Lakeview to Hobart Reservoir

Those who don't mind a stiff climb in exchange for a little solitude may enjoy the 5-mile, 2,500-foot climb to Hobart Reservoir, part of the municipal water system for Carson City tucked into the Marlette-Hobart backcountry of Lake Tahoe Nevada State Park. Along the way are numerous views of Washoe Valley and the surrounding hills, and once there, anglers and swimmers can enjoy their pursuits at the forest-rimmed lake. Plant lovers should appreciate the fine wildflower display in early season or the autumn foliage from quaking aspens in McEwen Creek Canyon.

LEVEL	Hike, advanced
LENGTH	10.0 miles, out and back
TIME	3/4 day
ELEVATION	+2,575'/−300'
USERS	Hikers, trail runners, mountain bikers, equestrians
DOGS	OK
DIFFICULTY	Strenuous
SEASON	June through October
BEST TIMES	June, early to mid-October
FACILITIES	None
MAPS	LTNSP: *Marlette-Hobart Backcountry* (http://parks.nv.gov /forms/Spooner_backcountry_map.pdf); USGS: *Carson City*
MANAGEMENT	Humboldt Toiyabe National Forest, Carson Ranger District at 775-882-2766, www.fs.usda.gov/htnf; Carson City Parks, Recreation, and Open Space at 775-887-2262, www.carson .org/government/departments-g-z/parks-recreation-open -space; Lake Tahoe Nevada State Park at 775-831-0494, www.parks.nv.gov/parks/marlette-hobart-backcountry/
HIGHLIGHTS	Autumn color, fishing, lake, stream, swimming, views, wildflowers
LOWLIGHTS	Steep

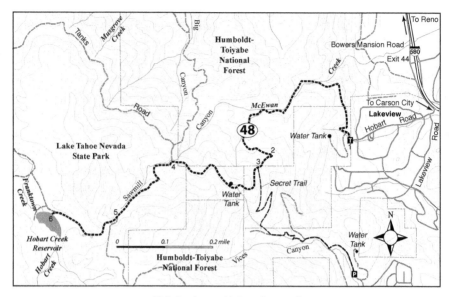

48. Lakeview to Hobart Reservoir

TIP | Stay on the alert for mountain bikers, as the Hobart Road is a relatively popular route with the two-wheel crowd heading into the Hobart-Marlette backcountry.

KID TIP | The full hike to Hobart Reservoir will be too much for most small children.

TRAILHEAD | 39°12.238'N, 119°49.042'W From Carson City, follow I-580 north toward Washoe Valley, and take the Eastlake Boulevard Exit 44. Turn left, pass under the freeway, and then turn left onto ALT 395. After 0.4 mile, turn right at Hobart Road and proceed through the Lakewood Estates subdivision for 0.75 mile to the end of paved road. Park your vehicle along the shoulder as space allows.

TRAIL | Beyond a closed steel gate, the route follows the continuation of the now dirt surface of Hobart Road, which bends sharply a couple of times while climbing stiffly through a light Jeffrey pine forest. Bitterbrush, manzanita, and sagebrush carpet the more open slopes where the trees start to thin. The open terrain allows for fine views of Washoe and Eagle Valleys below and across to the peaks of the Virginia Range. The grade eases for a while where the old road arcs around the hillside and bends into the canyon of McEwen Creek. You cross the willow- and cottonwood-lined stream, which passes through a pipe beneath the road. Climb upstream through strips of lush vegetation bordering the creek, including intermittent stands of quaking aspen. The steep road passes over the creek a few more times before it bends away and ascends across a hillside covered in sagebrush scrub, reaching a viewpoint [2] at a sharp turn at 2.25 miles from the trailhead. For anyone not up to the full hike to the reservoir, this viewpoint is a good turnaround point.

Continue climbing away from the viewpoint for a while to a junction [3] with the Secret Trail on the left, which descends into Vicee Canyon to Timberline Drive, and then proceed to a water tank and associated concrete-block building. Good views of Washoe Valley and bordering mountains continue along this stretch of road. Not far beyond the water tank, the grade mercifully eases on a 0.75-mile traverse across an open hillside toward Sawmill Canyon. A bounty of early-season wildflowers in this area includes lupine, mule ears, paintbrush, pennyroyal, and pentstemon. Reach a closed steel gate at the border of Lake Tahoe Nevada State Park, and then follow Sawmill Canyon Creek upstream to a junction, [4] 3.5 miles from the parking area, where little-used Tanks Road on the right heads across the creek and proceeds toward Red House.

Remaining on the main road, you veer left, pass an interpretive sign near an old steam engine, and enter a mixed forest of Jeffrey pines, white firs, and lodgepole pines. Keep ascending Sawmill Canyon, reaching a junction [5] at the crest of a low ridge, 4.5 miles from the trailhead. Here, a road on the left heads south for 0.75 mile to the Ash Canyon Road.

Go straight at the junction and make a moderate descent away from the ridge, soon catching a glimpse of Hobart Reservoir through brief gaps in the forest. Prior to the reservoir, you come to a sign with fishing regulations and statistical information. Just past the sign, follow a side road to the forest-rimmed shore. [6] When the time comes for your return, retrace your steps to the trailhead. [1]

WATER FOR THE COMSTOCK When the population of Virginia City and Gold Hill exploded during the mining boom, the need for water increased correspondingly, which required finding new sources. Herman Schussler designed a system to take water from the Carson Range down to the Lakeview saddle and then up to the Five Mile Reservoir near Virginia City, an engineering marvel at the time. From a dam on Hobart Creek, water was transported via box flumes to a pipeline. Increased pressure in the pipeline was sufficient to propel the water uphill to Virginia City. The twenty-one-mile-long project was completed in 1873 with a carrying capacity of 2.2 million gallons during a twenty-four-hour period. An additional flume and pipe system was built alongside the original two years later.

To satisfy the demand for even more water, in 1876 the Virginia and Gold Hill Water Company gained consent to take water from Marlette Lake after the dam was raised. Water from the lake was diverted into a flume and then sent through a tunnel built beneath the Carson Range. Once on the east side of the range, flumes carried the water to Hobart Creek and stored in the newly constructed Hobart Reservoir. A year later a third pressure pipeline was added to the system. After the end of the Comstock's heyday, the water system experienced a series of failures and ownership changes. Nowadays, the state of Nevada delivers water from the system to Virginia City and Gold Hill, Carson City, and Lakeview Estates.

MILESTONES

1: Start at Hobart trailhead; **2:** Viewpoint; **3:** Straight at Secret Trail junction; **4:** Left at junction with road to Red House; **5:** Straight at Ash Canyon Road junction; **6:** Hobart Reservoir; **1:** Return to trailhead.

GO GREEN I You can assist the Humboldt-Toiyabe National Forest by volunteering for a short-term or seasonal project. For more information, visit the volunteer page at www.fs.usda.gov/naub/r4/jobs/volunteer.

OPTIONS I Hikers will find the climb to Hobart Reservoir requires plenty of effort. Mountain bikers and trail runners have many alternatives for extending their trip on the fine network of roads in the Marlette-Hobart backcountry.

Secret Trail

One of the newest trails in Carson City, the Secret Trail is an important link in the area's network. While an unofficial trail existed here for years, recent trail-building improvements have greatly enhanced the former social trail that served as part of the route for Epic Ride's Carson City Off-Road mountain bike event. A new, three-quarter-mile section of single track now connects an old dirt road from Timberline Drive up a hillside to Hobart Road, where a fine view awaits. Once at Hobart Road, more adventurous hikers can extend the journey all the way to Hobart Reservoir.

LEVEL	Hike, advanced
LENGTH	9.5 miles, out and back to Hobart Reservoir; 8.0 miles, shuttle to Lakeview trailhead
TIME	3/4 day to Hobart Reservoir; 1/2 day to Lakeview trailhead
ELEVATION	+2,200'/−200'; +1,225'/−1,350'
USERS	Hikers, trail runners, mountain bikers, equestrians
DOGS	OK
DIFFICULTY	Moderately strenuous
SEASON	June through October
BEST TIME	June, early to mid-October
FACILITIES	None
MAPS	NSP: *Marlette-Hobart Backcountry* (http://parks.nv.gov/forms /Spooner_backcountry_map.pdf); USGS: *Carson City*
MANAGEMENT	Carson City Parks, Recreation, and Open Space at 775-887-2262, www.carson.org/government/departments-g-z/parks -recreation-open-space; Humboldt Toiyabe National Forest, Carson Ranger District at 775-882-2766, www.fs.usda.gov /htnf; Lake Tahoe Nevada State Park at 775-831-0494, www .parks.nv.gov/parks/marlette-hobart-backcountry/
HIGHLIGHTS	Autumn color, fishing, lake, stream, swimming, views, wildflowers
LOWLIGHTS	Steep

TIP | Stay on the alert for mountain bikers.

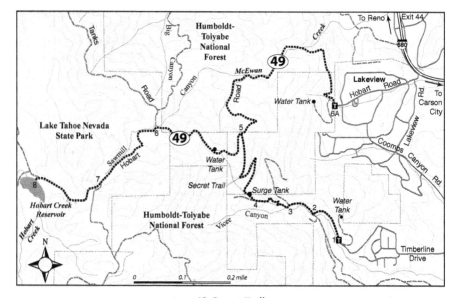

49. Secret Trail

KID TIP | Small children may find the climb a bit taxing.

TRAILHEAD | 39°11.276′N, 119°49.008′W From North Carson Street, turn west onto West College Parkway, and travel 0.7 mile to a right-hand turn onto North Ormsby Boulevard. Head north for 0.2 mile, and then turn left onto Coombs Canyon Road. Proceed another 0.7 mile to the intersection with Timberline Drive, go straight, follow Timberline for 1.4 miles to the end of the pavement, and park on the side of the road as space allows. If you have a high-clearance, 4WD vehicle, you may be able to drive another 1.2 miles to the end of the dirt road.

TRAIL | From the end of the pavement, walk up the dirt road above the north bank of Vicee Canyon. At 0.4 mile, veer to the right at a junction [2] and head northwest, continuing upstream through mostly open terrain. Follow the sometimes winding road up a sparsely forested hillside of Jeffrey pines for another 0.8 mile to the next junction. [3] Bend to the right at this junction, and climb along a dirt road for 0.2 mile to the end [4] near a surge pump on the Vicee Canyon water pipeline.

From the end of the road, single-track trail begins a steady upward traverse northeast across the mostly open hillside, with fine views down Vicee Canyon toward Carson City and the surrounding hills. Nearing a side canyon and a smattering of pines, the trail switchbacks and continues the upward journey arcing back toward the pipeline canyon before switchbacking again.

The climb continues into denser stands of timber upslope to a junction [5] with the Hobart Road, 2 miles from the end of the pavement. Here a fine view opens up to the north of Washoe Lake and Valley, which would be a fine turnaround point for those looking for a short out-and-back hike. If continuing beyond, there are a couple of options.

OPTION 1 TO HOBART RESERVOIR | From the Hobart Road junction, you turn left and proceed uphill to a water tank and associated concrete-block building. Good views of Washoe Valley and bordering mountains are continuous along this stretch of road. Not far beyond the water tank, the grade mercifully eases on a three-quarter-mile traverse across an open hillside toward Sawmill Canyon. A bounty of early-season wildflowers in this area includes lupine, mule ears, paintbrush, pennyroyal, and pentstemon. Reach a closed steel gate at the border of Lake Tahoe Nevada State Park, and then follow Sawmill Canyon Creek upstream to a junction, [4] a mile from the previous junction, where little-used Tanks Road on the right heads across the creek and proceeds toward Red House.

Remaining on the main road, you veer left, pass an interpretive sign near an old steam engine, and enter a mixed forest of Jeffrey pines, white firs, and lodgepole pines. Keep ascending Sawmill Canyon, reaching a junction [5] at the crest of a low ridge, 0.9 mile from the Tanks Road junction. The road on the left heads south for 0.75 mile to a connection with Ash Canyon Road.

Go straight at the junction and make a moderate descent away from the ridge, soon catching a glimpse of Hobart Reservoir through brief gaps in the forest. Prior to the reservoir, you come to a sign with fishing regulations and statistical information. Just past the sign, follow a side road to the forest-rimmed shore. [6]

OPTION 2 TO LAKEVIEW TRAILHEAD | With shuttle arrangements, you can head east toward the Lakeview trailhead (see Trip 48 for driving directions). From the Secret Trail / Hobart Road junction, [3] turn right and begin the stiff descent, soon emerging onto open, sagebrush-covered slopes with excellent views of the surrounding terrain and distant hills. Reach willow- and cottonwood-lined McEwen Creek, which you follow downstream and cross several times before the road veers away to the south. Follow the road as it wraps around a hillside at a more pleasant grade until a steeper, winding descent eventually leads to the trailhead. [4A]

GREENLEAF MANZANITA (*Arctostaphylos patula*) One of the most common shrubs in the chaparral community of the Great Basin and Sierra Nevada, greenleaf manzanita is certainly a common sight in the hills of the Carson Range. Spanning communities from the pinyon-juniper woodlands upward to 9,000 feet, this plant is easily identified by its

Greenleaf Manzanita blooms

bright green leaves and smooth, shiny, reddish-brown bark. In late spring and early summer, greenleaf manzanita bears clusters of distinct pinkish flowers.

MILESTONES (OPTION 1)

1: Start at end of pavement;   **2:** Turn right at junction;   **3:** Turn right at junction;   **4:** Reach end of road;   **5:** Hobart Road junction—turn left.

GO GREEN | Muscle Powered is the preeminent organization for building and maintaining trails in Carson City. Established in 1999, the group has been an unparalleled advocate for biking and hiking trails in the area. Along with trail building and maintenance, education, and advocacy, the nonprofit group also hosts community events. They routinely sponsor trash mobs, cleanup projects that provide a valuable asset to the beautification of the greater Carson City area. You can become a member and support the work at www .musclepowered.org.

OPTIONS | With a copy of the *Spooner Backcountry* map, the number of possible trip extensions is extensive.

Mount Davidson

A very steep climb on a sometimes rough road and a short cross-country section leads to an outstanding view from a rocky promontory above Virginia City, at 7,870 feet the highest point in the Virginia Range. Although the distance is short, the hike will seem longer than it is thanks to the stiff ascent. However, once the summit is gained and the stunning view unfolds, at least some of the labor fades from memory.

LEVEL	Hike, advanced
LENGTH	3.6 miles, out and back
TIME	1/2 day
ELEVATION	+1,500'/–0'
USERS	Hikers, trail runners
DOGS	OK
DIFFICULTY	Very strenuous
SEASON	All year*
BEST TIME	Spring, fall
FACILITIES	None
MAP	USGS: *Virginia City*
MANAGEMENT	Bureau of Land Management (BLM), Carson City District at 775-885-6000, www.blm.gov/office/carson-city-district-office
HIGHLIGHTS	Summit, views
LOWLIGHTS	Very steep

TIP | *Winter users may encounter snow en route to the top of Mt. Davidson, necessitating the use of traction devices or an ice axe, depending on conditions.

KID TIP | This extremely steep route is definitely not advised for young children. Older kids up to the task should bring plenty of fluids for the long and exposed climb.

TRAILHEAD | Follow SR 341 or SR 342 to Virginia City. In the middle of town, turn west at a flashing light onto Taylor Street, and proceed three blocks to where the road curves to the right and becomes Stewart Street. Immediately

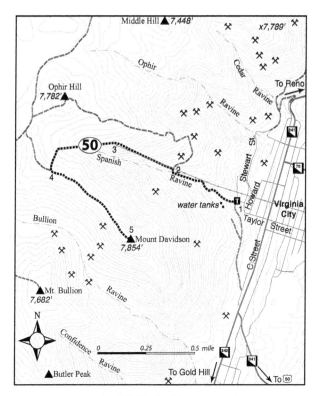

50. Mt. Davidson

take the first left onto Greg Street, and come to a small parking area just after the paved road bends sharply left (south-southwest). Parking should be available for about a half dozen vehicles.

TRAIL | From the parking area, walk a short distance back down Greg Street to the start of a dirt road heading steeply uphill toward Spanish Ravine. Climb stiffly up the ravine to where the road bends sharply to the right, crosses the ravine, and immediately reaches a junction [2] with a road on the left paralleling a utility line uphill.

Turn left and make an unrelenting, very steep climb toward the head of the canyon along the utility line, which runs just to the right of Spanish Ravine. Both the road and utility line terminate [3] well below the crest, where the route veers to the west and then south on a cross-country jaunt across open slopes of sagebrush scrub with very widely scattered junipers toward the top of the northwest ridge from Mt. Davidson. Reach the ridge crest and intersect a service road. [4]

View of Virginia City from Mt. Davidson

Turn left and follow the road on a much more pleasant grade along the crest past some communications equipment toward the base of Mt. Davidson, where a short but steep climb awaits. The road ends below the summit, which necessitates a short scramble over some rocks to gain the 7,854-foot summit. [5] As anticipated, the view is quite impressive in all directions. At the end of your stay, retrace your steps to the trailhead. [1]

VIRGINIA RANGE AND MOUNT DAVIDSON Unlike the typical north-south Nevada mountain range, the 30-plus-mile-long Virginia Range trends northeast to southwest. These mountains, volcanic in origin, tend to be more rounded and shorter than the typical Nevada variety as well. Located primarily within Storey County, the Virginia Range separates the two principal rivers in the area, the Truckee and Carson. As the range's and Storey County's highest summit, 7,870-foot Mt. Davidson towers over Virginia City. Prior to the current appellation, the mountain was named Sun Peak by early miners and later Mt. Pleasant. Although some minor disagreement exists, the prevailing opinion is the peak was named for Donald Davidson, the state geologist of California (who climbed the mountain).

1: Start at trailhead; **2:** Turn left at road; **3:** Turn left at end of utility line; **4:** Turn left at road; **5:** Summit of Mt. Davidson; **1:** Return to trailhead.

GO GREEN I Muscle Powered is the preeminent organization for building and maintaining trails in Carson City. Established in 1999, the group has been an unparalleled advocate for biking and hiking trails in the area. Along with trail building and maintenance, education, and advocacy, the nonprofit group also hosts community events. They routinely sponsor trash mobs, cleanup projects that provide a valuable asset to the beautification of the greater Carson City area. You can become a member and support the work at www .musclepowered.org.

OPTIONS I Peak baggers can knock off other nearby high points fairly easily, including Ophir Hill, Middle Hill, Cedar Hill, and Mt. Bullion.

Appendix: List of Abbreviations

LTNSP	Lake Tahoe Nevada State Park
NDOW	Nevada Division of Wildlife
NSP	Nevada State Parks
SR	State Route
TRT	Tahoe Rim Trail
USGS	US Geological Survey
USFS	US Forest Service

Index

Page numbers in italics refer to figures and photographs.

About the Author and Photographer

MIKE WHITE grew up in Portland, Oregon, from where he began adventuring in the Cascade Range. He obtained a BA from Seattle Pacific University, where he met and married his wife, Robin. The couple lived in Seattle for two years before relocating to Reno, where Robin had been accepted to medical school. For the next fifteen years, Mike worked for a consulting engineering firm, journeying to the Sierra Nevada and other western ranges as time permitted. During that time, the couple had two sons, David and Stephen, and Robin completed school and residency and then went into private practice as a pediatrician. On leaving the engineering firm, Mike started writing full time. A national award-winning author, Mike has contributed to numerous outdoor guides, including *Trinity Alps and Vicinity*, *Backpacking California*, *Backpacking Nevada*, *Top Trails: Lake Tahoe*, *50 Classic Hikes in Nevada*, *Afoot and Afield Reno-Tahoe*, *Lassen Volcanic National Park*, *Sequoia and Kings Canyon National Parks*, *Top Trails: Northern California's Redwood Coast*, *Top Trails: Sequoia and Kings Canyon National Parks*, *Best Backpacking Trips in California and Nevada*, and *Best Backpacking Trips in Utah, Arizona and New Mexico*. He also has written articles for magazines and newspapers. A former community college instructor, Mike is also a featured speaker for outdoors and conservation organizations.

MARK VOLLMER has shared his award-winning outdoor images through books, magazines, scenic calendars, gallery exhibits, multimedia slide shows, photo/music DVDs, and class instruction for thirty years. He believes that nature is often our greatest teacher—a deeper awareness of our natural surroundings and its seasonal rhythms translates to better photography. In turn, photography makes one a better naturalist. A resident artist with the Nevada Arts Council, Mark enjoys sharing his love of science, visual arts, and writing with school children and community audiences.